What the ange[ls] tell us now

Receiving, considering and acting on their messages

Irene Johanson

TEMPLE LODGE

Translated by Pauline Wehrle

Temple Lodge Publishing
Hillside House, The Square
Forest Row, East Sussex
RH18 5ES

www.templelodge.com

First published in English by Temple Lodge 2002

Originally published in German under the title *Was Engel uns heute mitteilen wollen, Ihre Botschaften wahrnehmen – bewegen – verarbeiten*, by Verlag Urachhaus, Stuttgart 2000

A catalogue record for this book is available from the British Library

ISBN 1 902636 30 9

Cover art by K. Martin-Kuri. Cover layout by S. Gulbekian
Typeset by DP Photosetting, Aylesbury, Bucks.
Printed and bound by Cromwell Press Limited, Trowbridge, Wilts.

Contents

Publisher's Note

This unique book is divided into two sections. The first part, based on Irene Johanson's many years' work as a priest, consists of her experiences of being attentive to angelic guidance. The second part of the book contains messages and information received through a friend whom she calls Agnes. As the author describes, Agnes represents a new kind of clairvoyance which does not entail a dimming of consciousness. Agnes' ability to communicate spiritually with the angelic world has the character of clarity and wakefulness.

Irene Johanson is a priest of the Christian Community, a church founded by Friedrich Rittelmeyer with the support of Rudolf Steiner (1861–1925). The Austrian-born Steiner, known today principally for the educational system he created — Steiner Waldorf education — was the founder of anthroposophy, a spiritual philosophy with a scientific basis. For the development of anthroposophy, Steiner founded the Anthroposophical Society. In contradistinction, the Christian Community was established primarily to renew religion and the Christian sacraments.

A small part of the contents of this book concerns esoteric questions directly connected to Rudolf Steiner's philosophy. In such instances background material is given, although it should be borne in mind that these are specialist and often quite technical issues. In addition, given that the book was written and first published in Germany, some passages relate specifically to Central European questions. For the sake of completeness, these passages have been retained in full for the English edition, and the text is fundamentally the same as in the original German.

Introduction

Some people nowadays, in clear daytime consciousness, receive messages from angels. They are able to be mediators for those whom angels want to approach in this way, as I was shown by grace in old age at the time when a mediator of this kind approached me on behalf of the angels.

I was greatly surprised by this, for I imagined I was very weak in the direction of spiritual efforts such as meditation and exercises for the treading of an inner path. I examined these messages extremely carefully to make sure I was not being dazzled by delusions. A criterion for the fact that these were 'good angels' was that they left me completely free. They told me neither what I should nor what I should not do, but just answered my questions.

It also happened that they withheld an answer for the sake of freedom. However, they also invited further questions 'because this is important both for you human beings and for us'.

I was struck by the constantly detectable closeness of the angel world, and could not understand why this was happening to *me*. Then I was told: 'All your life you have been open to angelic guidance. You were connected with us all the time, even though you did not know it. You were aware of it in the depths of your being when you told yourself and others: It is a matter of how we relate to ourselves. If we accept our own self and speak, act and think from out of that self, we can be in harmony with the angels.'

Then it suddenly dawned on me that this expression of identifying with oneself—realizing who you are—was the key to the door through which angelic guidance had come into my life as a human being.

It also became the key for this book.

What I shall be recounting here is the way human beings open doors to angels so that they can take part both in ordinary daily life and also in particularly important moments of destiny.

Part I

EXPERIENCES

Who am I?

Name and destiny

If someone else asks you who you are you will usually mention your name and possibly also where you live, what you do for a living and where you were born. You may be at a gathering where there are a lot of other people who are being briefly introduced to one another, and you exchange a few words or just see one another from a distance. On leaving, the one may say to the other: 'Happy to know you!' and the other might reply: 'You do not know me at all yet!'

To get to know another person more is needed than just knowing a name and seeing his or her external form. We need to know ourselves and be able to live with the question: Who am I?

We do not need to have arrived at a conclusive answer, but it is important to follow up the question if we are to understand another person and recognize connections of destiny, complications, omissions, and inner growth.

Who am I? This question is about myself and at the same time it is the key to the world. I have to accept myself first, and then I can accept the world. 'Love your neighbour as yourself.' Who am I myself, that I can love myself and my neighbour as myself? Who am I?

First of all there is the name I was given by others at the beginning of my earthly life, and which I am called by. Even a small child feels it is being referred to when it hears its name spoken. Before it says I to itself it says its name, addressing itself as though it were someone else. This is an indication that it is still fully identical with the supersensible being with whom it has prepared its destiny and is continuing to work. The child itself has planned and initiated its destiny, which is in harmony with its own angel and other people's, and which determines the family into which it will be born, the time and place of birth, and the particulars of nationality and the spirit of the age. Very often in the birth constellation a motif is struck which will resound throughout life. People born into a large family often have to cope until the end of their lives with strong family ties and a large amount of family karma. Yet nowadays there are also many people who are brought up as the only child of a single parent. They often seek out a family situation outside the blood tie. In later life such people can develop the ability to cultivate spiritual relationships, create social communities.

Variations on the theme of Homelessness

I was born to very young parents. My father was still studying when a child was expected. He took the young mother abroad. The child was born there, and in the absence of a real home she travelled with her parents from one place of study and one temporary stopping place to another. In the first years of her life her parents' love was her home. They were her anchor in a foreign country, in this homelessness. When the child was four years old her father emigrated, separated from the mother, and took the child to strangers. There, she grew up with her sister and some other children, surrounded by loving care, in the midst of unspoilt nature and in a broad-minded, openhearted atmosphere. The child accepted this situation without question. She took it for granted. This kind of acceptance is the secret of such a childhood: the being of the child, whilst still dreamy and immature where life on earth is concerned, realizes its true nature, identifies with itself in that it enters into its destiny as something which belongs to it. In this state of total acceptance we as human beings live under the guidance of our angel. Thus right from childhood home-lessness was my homeland. This still continued when this home was dissolved by the Nazis. I now had to take a further step into the sphere of homelessness. I was put in a denominational boarding-school. It was all strange to me, and I was put off religion by the school's abuse of it. The only bit of home that remained to me was my sister. When this establishment was closed I left the country for a year with my sister and we rejoined our mother at her place of work. Now we suddenly lived in the kind of freedom we had never known before, for neither our mother nor the teacher were an authority for us German children abroad. This childhood freedom, consisting of being able to give yourself up to the moment, not having anybody or anything that could force you to do anything, was for a whole year like a home amidst the homelessness. We then went back to Germany. As a fourteen-year-old I had to leave secondary school because I was a 'Jewish half-caste of the first order'. I was taken in by a family we were friendly with, so that I could do my compulsory year of service, but the village organizer of the department made a complaint against the father of the family because, as a lieutenant commander, he had allowed his children to be taught by a person who was half Jewish. So I could not stay there any longer. My mother and also my grandmother were both in a sanatorium seriously ill with TB. The remaining relatives had taken my sister in and did not want to burden themselves with a second 'half-caste'.

Now, for the first time, I saw homelessness as a state of being abandoned, pushed out — as a disaster. The state of being in tune with angels and thus being able to accept the homelessness as a natural condition appeared to have broken down. There was suddenly no room for me in this world any more; I did not belong anywhere. But deep down I was carried by the assurance that this destiny, which was so difficult to bear, was part of it all and belonged to me. I might have been abandoned by the world, but the angels had not deserted me. One bit of help followed another. A place of service was found for me. Then I was released to care for my mother. I took every opportunity to learn something and to get to know interesting people. Thus I was able to hear lectures by Professor Eugen Herrigel, the author of the book *Zen in the Art of Archery* (Arkana 1988), although I was far too young. Homelessness opened up for me the world of past spirituality. I took unexpected events for granted again. I knew nothing about angels, yet without knowing it I gave myself up to their guidance in that I accepted my life as it was and learnt from everything. I wanted to learn as much as I could. I was still a child, for only children can be so unquestioning, can enter into a difficult destiny with so little grumbling and complaining, and be at the same time both passive and active. It is precisely this eagerness to learn combined with submission to destiny that points to the participation of angels in the life of a growing child. The question is no longer: Who am I? but is part of life. 'This is me!'

Wresting creative power from the abyss

Between the karmic circumstances connected with birth and the beginning of puberty children's relation to the world of the angels changes in many ways according to the unconscious strength of their connection with their destiny.

A five-year-old boy felt the irresistible urge to paint pictures of horrible cruelty, even murder, torture and the
Crucifixion. This was despite the fact that his parents protected him from anything that might have contributed to
this urge. There was no TV, no horror stories, no illustrated
papers. It was as though the child's soul absorbed in the
night all the horrors of the city, and during the day he had
to rid himself of them again. One day the boy asked his
parents, who were not church-goers, if he might go to the
Sunday children's service with his sister who was of school
age. Both his parents and the priest thought he was too
young and should wait until he had entered the big school,
but he had his way. He absorbed the simple images of the
ritual, and asked for them every Sunday. It was not long
before the urge to paint horrible things subsided. It was as
though a protective cloak of true images from the world of
the angels had been put around him, so that the pictures
from the abyss could no longer enter his soul. This double
process, of being released from the influences of the abyss
in turning towards sources of creativity wherever they were
to be found, became his life's motif. In his vocation as a
saxophonist he had ever and again to experience the pull
between these two worlds. Over and over again he had to
wrest creativity from the abyss, and come in this way to the
experience of: Who am I? This wrestling which, even as a
child, drew him towards the Christ, and gave him the
opportunity to experience the world of the angels, determined his whole further life.

Dealing with children's trust

Every child in the ninth year of life has a special experience
of the question: Who am I? Children begin to compare

themselves with others. My friend is better at arithmetic than I am. I have more friends than he has. Or the puzzling question arises: Why am I not my sister? Why is my sister not me? We wonder whether the grown-ups are fair. Do they themselves do what they expect me to do? Can I believe them? Do they have any idea what they are talking about when they speak to me about God or angels?

A boy was still romping around in bed long after he should have been asleep. His mother told him off to no avail. Then she went so far as to say: 'If you won't calm down at once your guardian angel will not come tonight.' To which the eight-year-old replied: 'I am sick of the sound of his wings anyway.' A situation such as this shows that children lose their connection with angels if their parents misuse it, if their parents lose their credibility and do not stand up to the tests their children put them through. Children would dearly like to trust adults and see them as thoroughly truthful and in possession of unfailing integrity. They feel let down if the adult does not live up to their hopes and expectations.

As a religion teacher there was an occasion when I was telling nine-year-olds the story of Moses leading his people through the desert and of how, despite all the set-backs and shortcomings of the people, he kept his trust in the guidance of God. Then one of the girls asked me: 'Do you have the same sort of trust in God as Moses had?' The question went straight to my heart. How should I reply? I felt the child's expectations. I felt I had to tell her the truth. And I could not tell her at her age that I would have to think about it, for the moment called for a decisive 'yes!' or 'no!'. So I said 'Yes!' And as soon as I had said it I felt I had made a promise to that girl's angel. Whenever in later life I felt doubts approaching, that 'Yes' arose in me again. I wanted to have told the girl the truth. She and I had given one another an angelic promise.

A picture of the destiny belonging to the next step in life

Some children balk at having to take this step which the world confronts them with. There was a boy of this age who was still a playful dreamer and did not want to accept that thoughtless play could harm others. He thought it was fun to pull the chair away from a child who was about to sit down, and who then fell over backwards. And he actually injured a child in this way. His games were often dangerous to others because he did not stop to think but got carried away by the fun of it.

So his angel took direct action. The boy went to the circus with his siblings. In the interval he wanted to look at the wild animals in their cages. The lions had cubs. A rope cordoned off the area, so that no-one would get too close to the animals. But the boy slipped under the rope and stood directly in front of the cage. A lion cub wanted to play with him, stuck its paw through the bars and tore a deep gash down one side of his face and body. He was taken to hospital. I visited him there and said to him: 'You know, this accident could only have happened to you. Other children get run over or fall off a wall or come to grief while ski-ing. You have been hurt by a lion cub who only wanted to play with you. You yourself are just like that lion cub. You only want to play, and it does not bother you if another child gets hurt by it.'

This experience woke the child up, and he became a nine-year-old who asked himself: Who am I? This restored him to a state of harmony with his environment. The way some people look at a similar situation is that they often say: The guardian angel was not paying attention when this accident happened. In actual fact this sort of thing is really intended by the angel because the human being needs this so-called accident. Removing his protection from the boy so that he could be wounded by the lion was an act of love on the part of the angel to get him to take the necessary step.

Understanding twelve-year-olds with the help of the wisdom of angels

Some children break away from angelic guidance at an early age. A twelve-year-old boy, together with his bike, became entangled with a car and was hurled through the air right across the street. He hit the ground hard, yet he only received a few grazes and no broken bones, bruises or concussion. Then only a few days later he climbed a tree and fell, receiving a multiple wrist fracture and two injured vertebrae. He had to lie still for a long time. His parents were worried, and they asked what it could signify that their son came away so lightly the first time and was seriously hurt subsequently. Might there perhaps be a connection between the boy's accident and his quarrelsome attitude to his younger sister? Or had they, as parents, done something wrong in his upbringing? I arranged that the young woman should ask the angels, and we were told: 'The boy has sent his guardian angel away. This does not happen as seldom as you might think. This is why the injury could happen. In the case of the car accident his angel checked the fall. But the boy does not want this protection. He wants to take on responsibility for his own actions. He is afraid; afraid of life, of growing up, of having to make decisions and having to be responsible. On the other hand everything is pushing him to determine situations for himself. But when it comes to the crunch he is still much too much of a child. This serious injury shows that he relies too much on himself, and wants to take on too much responsibility. He is overtaxing himself, will no longer allow himself to be a child. The situation makes his parents feel helpless, and all they can do is watch this lonely battle. They ought to leave the child, the "little adult", in peace. Do they love him as he is, and accept him for what he is? The most important feeling for him now is that his parents accept him, even if he no longer likes himself. Is this possible? The boy is described as difficult. Yet all he needs is his parents' forebearance and love. To feel secure and to be set free. Too much stress is laid on his difficult relationship with his younger sister. In the higher worlds the two of them chose this sibling constellation to balance out old karma. Perhaps they will come to remember this and do something about their pre-natal intention. There is still more of their life to come. The exchanges between them have not yet come to an end. It lays a great strain on the parents, but where the children are concerned it is very important that they know that karmic relationships begin even among siblings. These sibling constellations are a special form of this relationship. It binds them so strongly in the early years. You have to keep on encountering this person who is so close to you. In adult life one simply keeps out of their way. This is what sibling constellations are like — for a certain time they are unavoidable.'

This message, though given to a particular couple, contains truths which, with modifications, apply to many children of this age. Rudolf Steiner once said that a human being's personal destiny begins at the age of twelve. This has something to do with the fact that the relation between young people and their angel changes. They come into conflict, as it says in the message. They no longer want to be protected, but as yet they do not have the strength to go it alone. They lose their childlike way of identifying with their own self, yet it is precisely in this loss that their identity lives, for it belongs to them and their pre-natal karmic will. Time and again spiritual reality is a paradox. In losing, at the threshold from childhood to youth, the way they identify with their own self—the feeling of unison they have with their angel—this is exactly when young people take a step their angel recognizes, and begin their personal destiny. When they free themselves from their angel the angel is close to them and lives in this liberation.

This is why on the one hand we experience the early part of youth as a time full of joy, ideals, discoveries, enthusiasm and love, yet on the other hand as such a difficult time, full of loneliness, abysses and inner distress. For this is the time when the young person's angel leaves him or her free, with all the risks that belong to any area of freedom. This is what angelic guidance means. This is portrayed in a legend which corresponds particularly to this age:

From out of the spiritual world a human being looks down at his life, which looks to him like a journey through the desert. In the sand he sees two sets of footprints and realizes that one set belongs to him and the other to his angel. He notices that each time he was in special trouble, danger and difficulty there was only one set of footprints to be seen. He asks his angel why he left him by himself at the most difficult times, for corresponding with each of those occasions only one pair of footprints is to be seen. The angel replies: 'My child, that was when I carried you.' What is experienced on earth as a desertion by the angel is a time when one is being carried in spirit!

The effect on the young of souls who die early

If a person is removed from the earth by death at an early age it can happen that he or she takes on a mission similar to an angel. A death of this kind is deeply upsetting for people. But precisely because this is so it opens up their souls like a plough does the soil, and they become capable of receiving the seeds of what they perceive to be clear signs of destiny, purposeful guidance from those dead souls of the kind which otherwise comes from angels.

A seventeen-year-old girl died completely unexpectedly a very short time after suddenly having kidney failure. During the three days between her death and her funeral her friends, class mates, all those close to her, felt the need to get together and remember her, and to round off this gathering by doing something to raise their personal pain on to a level beyond the personal. They lit candles and prayed that the early death of this girl might not have been in vain. When the three days were over their longing to connect with the dead soul and to include her in earthly life did not diminish. Before every festival they organized a service in which they endeavoured to reflect on the nature of the Christian festivals and to bring them alive again in the present. They did this regularly for a year. Then a few of them met in a smaller circle and told one another of the occasions when they had felt their dead friend to be near them. She had helped them chiefly with making decisions. The most important thing about this was the certainty it gave them that souls who die young remain united with the life of those on earth, that they can be consciously included, and that the people still on earth can rediscover through them that angels exist.

One of the girls told us that she had been faced with deciding whether to form a lifelong union with a particular man. In the evening, before falling asleep, she had heard within her, spoken quite loudly and clearly in her friend's voice, the words: Do not do it! Instantly she knew it was her angel speaking to her through the dead girl. She thought the whole matter through again, and suddenly realized that deep down she already knew what had been confirmed in that way. Through that early death those young people were given an openness for the spirit which, through all the ups and downs of life, has never quite left them since. There are many such examples. They contribute to making people accessible once more to the angel world, and to bringing more light and transparency into the hard and dark layers which have, with the advancing centuries, been separating human souls more and more from the world of spirit beings.

Finding oneself in the course of taking an interest in the world

It is typical of the way young people progress in the early years that they do not ask: Who am I? but are interested in what is going on in the world, what other people are thinking and going through, how people of other nationalities do things, what the world used to be like and how it has changed, how technology works or simply how one can be a contemporary person. Whilst making all these discoveries young people are no longer led by their angel. Unconsciously they are aware of being abandoned, and so they put themselves in the hands of the group being of their generation, or of the spirituality living in it. They give themselves up to the negative or positive being of their time, until one day the question once more arises: Who am I? This occurs with some young people at the age of eighteen, with others later. Yet it always takes place through a meeting.

After having begun my life with the motif of homelessness I came into contact when I was seventeen with people who had been active as social workers from out of an understanding of the human being based on Rudolf Steiner's anthroposophy. Most of this was still mentally way beyond my understanding, yet I knew at once that this was what I wanted. This belongs to me. This calls me. This is at the root of my life. This is me. For the first time I was conscious of my identity, so I could again experience that the angel world guided me here on earth. Where the other people in my environment were concerned I became a new person. The quiet, reserved, dreamy girl became lively, purposeful and full of initiative. Despite my four years without any schooling I took my school-leaving exam a year later. When two school friends of mine visited me at home they told my mother what her daughter had got going in the class; for instance I had started a choir which performed at school festivals. My mother could hardly believe they were talking about her daughter, for she had noticed none of this transformation. For this familiar home was not my true home. I now found that my true home was where the events of life had a quality of wonder in the true sense of the word, where they brought about miracles.

The kind of thing that happened was that a young girl who had seen me at a lecture spoke to me in the tram. She told me that until school began again she had a group of children coming to her home to whom she was giving Waldorf education, and would I like to come and see what was going on. I was of course very happy to do so. The experience sparked off in me the resolve to work with children in this way later on. Through the same girl I got to know the lady who nine months later became the headmistress of my secondary school. I discussed with her which class I should be in after missing four years of school. The answer was: 'You will go into the class corresponding to your own age, the one I shall be taking, and do your exams in a year's time.' And that is what happened. This lady also told me about a circle of young people at the Christian Community, a religious movement which, like Waldorf education, had arisen with the help of Rudolf Steiner. I went to it, and from then on my interest, love, thirst for knowledge and my activity was centred almost entirely round the Christian Community. The strokes of destiny and guidance which I had had confirmed that this was the path for me. Because buses did not run in the evenings I walked the six kilometres home after an event in town several times a week. I lived in the country. Our neighours asked my mother whether she was not anxious about her daughter constantly having to walk past the barracks alone, where young girls were always being molested. To which my mother replied: 'My daughter is not afraid, therefore I am not afraid either.' On one occasion after a New Year's Eve sermon I wanted to turn a different way and take the road through a valley. When the tram had brought me to the terminus I clearly had the feeling that on this particular evening I should not walk home. So I turned round and knocked on my teacher's door. She was willing to take me in at once and put me up for the night. Two days later the local paper told us that on that New Year's Eve two women had been attacked by drunkards in that valley.

I also got to know my most important teachers and friends by means of strokes of destiny. For instance at one time I wanted to attend a youth conference in Holland, but I did not get a visa. I was deeply disappointed and sad about having to remain in Germany. Then I heard about a conference in the Sauerland which had already started. I went nevertheless, and got to know someone there who was giving a painting course. He helped me overcome the preconceived idea drummed into me at school that I could not paint. This man became my teacher both where the experiencing of nature was concerned and also the experiencing of destiny. My deep connection with him lasted until his death and beyond. I did indeed give thanks for the circumstances which had hindered me from going to Holland. It was not until much later that I became conscious that behind all such strokes of destiny angels are at work. I was at peace with myself, I was absolutely conscious of the way I was going, and this was at the same time the path along which my angel was guiding me. I was in harmonious accord with the path of destiny which I, as a human being before birth, had chosen to follow.

Recognizing one's pre-natal resolves

This resolve to follow one's self-chosen destiny is sometimes perceived by other intuitive people much earlier than by oneself. It is not until we awaken to our own being around the twenty-first year that we experience the confirmation of what others sense at an earlier date and which has been accompanying us unconsciously throughout our childhood and youth.

A child of a middle-class family was baptised by a Christian minister of the church who was a well-known Indian and Buddhist scholar. After the christening he told the child's parents: Your child will one day build a bridge between East and West. The boy was the only child of those parents, and it was unpleasant for them to imagine that their son might some day live a long way away from them. They therefore told the boy nothing about the minister's words.

When at the age of five the child caught the word 'Japan' being mentioned in an adult conversation he exclaimed: 'Japan! That is where I belong!' His father told him that he did not have the faintest idea where Japan was. This irritated the boy, and he said no more. But when he was thirteen he began to learn Japanese. After taking his school-leaving exam he got a job at the Japanese embassy. The first time he went to Japan he noticed immediately the truth of what he had said as a young child. He became the first European master in the Zen Buddhist tea ceremony. Returning to Germany after this he informed his parents that he had accepted the call to join the Waseda University in Tokyo and take his place there as professor of German until he was seventy. Not until they were taking leave of him at the station did his parents tell him what the minister had told them at his christening.

His destiny now began to be fulfilled, and the young man totally identified with it. He made a deep connection with Japanese culture and with the roots of that people. As an individual he had no doubt about already being connected with those roots. In his present lifetime he brought to Japanese culture a kind of Christianity which acknowledges the spiritual elements inherent in Buddhism, and he conveyed to Europeans the kind of Buddhism which had progressed since Buddha's times in the spirit of Christ's ongoing activity. As a confirmed Christian he became a Buddhist priest. This was the way he experienced his identity, which at the time of his baptism had already been perceived by the minister who baptised him. Angel guidance reaches way beyond the frontiers of any confession. That was the unspoken message of this earth life.

Recognizing strokes of destiny to be pre-natal resolves

A person can also identify with a tragic destiny. A group of fifteen-year-olds were rehearsing Hugo von Hofmannsthal's *Das Salzburger Grosse Welttheater* with me. In it Lady World calls down the unborn souls and gives them the roles they have to play on earth. There is a proud man, a modest one, a dancer, a merchant, a king and a beggar. The soul who is meant to be a beggar refuses to take on the role. He recoils at such a life. Eventually though, he submits to destiny. When, at the end of their lives, the other actors encounter death coming to collect them, they all protest. The beggar is the only one who welcomes him as a friend.

The boy playing the role of the beggar was exceptionally gifted. And he threw himself heart and soul into the part. During the performance it shot through my mind that he was acting out his own destiny. Another member of the audience had the same thought. But we pushed the idea to the back of our minds. I did not remember it again until, when he was twenty-one, he contracted Bechterew's disease, an illness in which the spine stiffens bit by bit. The person can only take short steps. In his case there was also hyper-sensitivity of the senses and of the inner organs. The young man withdrew entirely from his family and also from society as a whole. Wherever he appeared he was condemned as a beggar and an outcast. He could only stand or lie but not sit down. Sometimes, if he lay down on the seat in the underground train an official would order him out. People laughed at him. Mothers warned their children against him. Girl friends would not stick by him. Although he was adequately covered by a disability pension his life was like that of a beggar where love, understanding and acceptance were concerned. The amazing part of it is that the man accepted the life of a beggar and learnt to live with this condition which gave him unspeakable bodily pain. Even if he might not have formulated it this way, what he was doing was constantly working at learning to identify with his destiny and confirming his own pre-natal acceptance of it.

Threshold experiences

There are shocking answers, too, to the question: 'Who am I?' We prefer to avoid them or make light of them. And yet these experiences are essential if, in our further life, we want to be in harmony with ourselves and, with the help of our angel, find and co-operate with this realm. It is a threshold experience. When we go through this we have moments when we see ourselves from the other side of the threshold which we, as earth citizens, experience as existing between the sense world and the supersensible world. One should not bring this experience about artificially, e.g. by psychoanalytical methods. For one must be mature enough if one is to do it in a wholesome way. No-one can assess this maturity from outside, and some of the people who have been transported by a humanly-contrived method into the depths and shallows of their own soul thereby become dependent and angst-ridden or arrive at a permanent state of pre-occupation with themselves. However, those who let life itself bring them to self-observation, and then stand firm, will find that from then on they confront life differently. They no longer need merely to think about or believe in the reality of spiritual beings, for now they find them to be actually present in the earthly realm because, from time to time at least, they can now experience the world as a totality.

What are such meetings with oneself like? Certainly they are very individual and vary in every case. What is applicable in general can be made clearer by particular examples. I received a penalty ticket because, on removing my car from a parking space, I had rammed another car without leaving my address or that of my insurance. As it was a business car the ticket was addressed to my place of work. I found this extremely embarrassing. Then I discovered I had no knowledge of the street in which the event had occurred and that for the particular time in question I had an entry in my diary for a visit to a sick friend. I clung to these two facts with relief, and was convinced that the ticket was a mistake and that I was innocent. So I dismissed it. A little while later, on visiting the sick friend again, I discovered that in the street where he lived there was a ban on parking. So I found a parking space in a side street. My eye fell on the street name-plate. It was the very name of the one on my penalty ticket. And suddenly I saw the whole scene before me. The cars behind and in front of me had been very close to mine. I had heard a gentle scraping sound, and had driven off without looking round. Something in me had not wanted to admit the fact, and so I had pushed it away behind my explanations.

As I became conscious of all this it was as though a curtain burst apart before my inner eye and an abyss opened up before my soul. This is impossible to describe with earthly concepts and processes. All the evil of it, the injustice, the baseness and meanness appeared before me as one huge and terrible image, and with it the shattering, shameful recognition: That is me! Then, however, I experienced the truth of what had until then been only a meaningless religious expression, that in this abyss is the Being who bears the sins of the world. This was the other side belonging to that experience. Yet this Being did not appear from outside, or speak to me from the abyss, but out of my own inner being there came the words: 'I am your I. This ego am I.' This experience brought with it an intensified readiness to accept myself, however painful, embarrassing or difficult it might be. When something like this happens a positive space is always created for the angels participating in a human destiny to reach the person whom they would not have been able to reach without it. For they do not storm into a human life like despots or fanatics, but knock at the door, and enter only if their knock is heard and they are granted entry.

Facing up to one's own weaknesses

I had to go through test after test where facing up to myself was concerned. I gave religion lessons to a great many age groups. In the course of the years I had acquired so much experience with children and young people that I believed that nothing would throw me any more and I would be able to cope with any teaching situation.

Then one day I took over a sixth class. It started off well, but then I experienced the children slipping more and more out of my control. I was eventually right at my wits' end and totally worn out. Every lesson went wrong. I was desperate. There were a number of possible explanations. The class had had a great many changes of teacher. The other teachers also had great trouble with them. A lot of the children were from broken marriages. But none of these explanations made the situation any better. Eventually I considered whether I should hand the class over the following year to a colleague who might manage them better than I did. In the course of thinking these thoughts I suddenly realized that this might all have something to do with me. Was I not just about reaching the point of considering myself pedagogically infallible? Didn't I think I was the cat's whiskers? Didn't I need to be brought down a peg or two, so that humility would replace pride? I accepted the lesson given me by the angel of destiny and kept the class. And from that moment on I had no more difficulties with those children. I kept them right through to class 12, and I maintained a good relationship with a number of them even after they had left school. I thought of this class as my 'cross', my destiny, for they had enabled me to have an important experience in the direction of identifying with myself. I could face up to my own weaknesses, and children and young people, who have a strong sense for what is 'real', appreciate this above all other educational accomplishments.

For instance, one day I remarked to an upper school pupil I met in the playground: 'You have the knack of disturbing any lesson with your brief, cynical remarks, especially when the others are in a particularly thoughtful and heartfelt mood. I do not know how I can prevent this, and simply do not know what to do. Can you possibly suggest anything?' To which he said: 'I do not actually do it deliberately. It always just comes over me. The special atmosphere irritates me, and I have to say something silly. Do you know what? Let's choose a code word. Say quite casually, but in my direction: "Let me see." And I will keep a hold on myself.' I followed his advice, and it worked well. After a little while I did not need to say it any longer. It was as though the young man had been freed from a spell, and he could open up to those special moments. But do your utmost to avoid applying this sort of thing deliberately, with the intention of achieving a result. The aspect of being at a loss and speaking to the pupil must only come from communing with yourself and not be used merely as a trick of the trade. Unless this is so the helping spirits cannot participate.

Identifying with one's position or office

People who wear an official hat, who play a role in society or take a leading part in a particular province find it especially difficult to act, speak or think from out of themselves. This is evident through the fact that they refer to their varying attitudes with the words: I am now in an official capacity, and: I am now a private individual. We all have different ways of speaking and behaving towards other people according to how we relate to them. We speak differently according to whether the other person is our spouse, or our boss, a friend or confidant, a person down on his luck or someone on top of the world, a child, or someone at death's door. A priest speaks differently if he is directing himself to the world of the spirit in the course of a service, or has a large congregation in front of him, than he does when he is holding a conversation with one person or only a few people. These differences go to show that we can speak from out of ourselves in a great many ways because we are taking the situation into account, involving ourselves with it and admitting that something is finding expression that lives between us and others. We and another person can unite in this intermediate area without losing or denying ourselves. Every community, marriage, school class or working team has this 'shared area'. We call it the class spirit, the spirit of the business, the house spirit, the angel of the community. In its service, despite all the changes of behaviour, I can always be myself.

Yet when we say: I am now a doctor, teacher, priest or chef, and in a while I shall be a private person, our office is like a hat we put on and take off, and people are conscious of this hat. The impression we make is by means of our attire and not through what we ourselves are. We imagine we only re-appear as ourself when we are in a private situation, e.g. among our family. Then the opposite extreme often applies. At last we can let ourselves go, do what we feel like doing, take off our hat and be as we imagine we really are. But is this really who we are? After all, we are letting ourselves go — we are taking leave of ourself — and we are not present in that sort of behaviour. Holidays are then called 'having a break from my ego'. But it is not your own ego at all that is the active agent either in the official role or in the letting-go as a private person. What is at work here is a mistaking of the soul for the ego. When in office one should give up being personal or subjective; but that is one's soul and not one's individuality. One should not, for instance, allow one's sympathies and antipathies to enter into what one does where working with patients, pupils and clients is concerned. One should not let one's state of soul loose on other people. And the other way round: the other people should be able to meet with the official's ego being and not merely the official. The ego lives in a rhythm of opening to the other person and coming to itself. We open ourselves to our official duty, and our ego being lives in this opening up gesture; in fact this is where its presence is particularly felt. And the other gesture is not 'letting oneself go' but 'coming to oneself'. This 'concentration of self' is the soil for a new impulse of opening up.

If people want to avoid succumbing to the illness of our time, which is a splitting up in all the different spheres of life, then they should not separate themselves into officials and private persons. They must enter fully into each situation, whether it is a professional one, an intimate one or a holiday one and, working out of the impression made by what they have experienced and learnt, they must come to themselves and let this work on them. Then they will always continue to have the experience of being themselves. It is in this breathing space in the centre of the pendulum swing that the angel can be active. Then not only do children learn from their teacher but the teacher also learns from the children, the doctor from the patient, and the priest from the confessional. So-called private life also breathes in this rhythm, and gives entry to the angel, even when or especially when life goes through crises. For in no way do angels want to prevent crises; that is precisely when they want to make themselves felt. It is when we cannot find our way on our own that they send us pointers, give us strength, and comfort or caution us.

What is that telling me?

Nature as a language of the spirit

Those who wish to include the world of the angels in their life must learn to let circumstances tell them things. You can begin doing this by practising on nature, especially plants. If you look at a daisy closely and follow it through the course of its day and its year, you can learn a lot from it. It emerges from the earth very early in the year and forms a long stem, leaving its rosette of leaves behind on the ground. Its blossom is a tiny yellow sun from which a ring of white petals ray out. This blossom opens to the touch of the first rays of the sun and closes when the sun disappears. During the day this blossom follows the path of the sun. In late autumn, when all the other flowers have disappeared, you can still see the odd daisy in the meadow, its white blossom like a messenger of light in the grey of November. Through careful watching you can get this little flower to speak to you. The words, coming from the story of God's creation, are these: The great sun awakens in me a spark of sun. My blossom remains united with the sun, accompanies him throughout the day and the year, and closes when the sun disappears and goes to shine on other creatures. I open to the sun as soon as it returns again. When I close because it is no longer shining on me, I preserve its power within me to form more and more new blossoms. I withdraw into the earth for only a short time in winter. There the force of the sun works on me invisibly, forms me anew in its image, which I then bring to manifestation again in the visible world.

When we listen to the heavenly being of the plant speaking to us from out of its earthly form, we feel that there is a kinship in us with this small flower. But first of all we must make it real. We have to find our own spiritual sun. Its light is knowledge and its warmth is love, and both of these take effect in creative human activity. Knowing, loving and creating are the forces of the sun of Christ, which create their image in every human soul — the Christ-related human ego — which bursts into blossom each time we are truly ourself, and which stays alive throughout the day and the year even when we feel far away from the world of God and shut ourself off from our environment. Indeed, according to Friedrich Schiller, every plant has something to tell us: 'If you want to find the exalted source of all greatness, the plants can instruct you, for what the plant is through no will of its own you can be with deliberate intention.' Invisible beings speak to us even through visible plants if we are able to hear the visible world as a language speaking to us of the realm of the supersensible.

Angelic messages through natural occurrences

There are times, too, when nature says something to us in absolutely personal situations. Nature becomes the mediator of an angelic message.

I was called to the bedside of a young man with cancer, who was fighting for his life but knew in his subconscious that he was dying. In such life situations it is always extremely difficult to find the right moment for the last sacrament. The dying person must be ready for it and feel, themselves, that they are on the threshold. It should not happen too soon, nor should the right moment be missed.

Questions of this kind were in my mind as I drove out of town through fields and meadows to the sick man.

Suddenly I saw in the sky a cloud formation resembling a human profile, in fact it reminded me somewhat of the face of the patient. The mouth was partly open and out of it rose a delicate cloud shaped like an elf. Then I knew that the young man would soon breathe his last. When I arrived he was fully prepared to receive the sacrament. And only a few hours later he died.

Nature and art

To understand the message which is trying to reach us through the particular situation of a natural occurrence requires creative activity, a kind of transforming of the picture into actual human life. This can be practised using plants as examples. They show us archetypal images of the human soul and its activities. People who have woken up by this means to everything that speaks in the world can be told much more than people who close themselves to such communication either because they are too apathetic and inflexible in their soul or because they consider such things to be chance, illusion or actually non-existent. They refuse to get involved, and they bar the way to the invisible messengers who want to speak to them through nature. Those people who do allow them in, however, will acquire access to the language previously closed to them, the language of the word of God, which is always at one and the same time both personal and universally human.

The artist Alexey Jawlenski illustrated this in his 'meditations'. Reduced to a minimum of lines and colours they present both a window with cross-bars and a human countenance. With each picture he painted Jawlenski had a

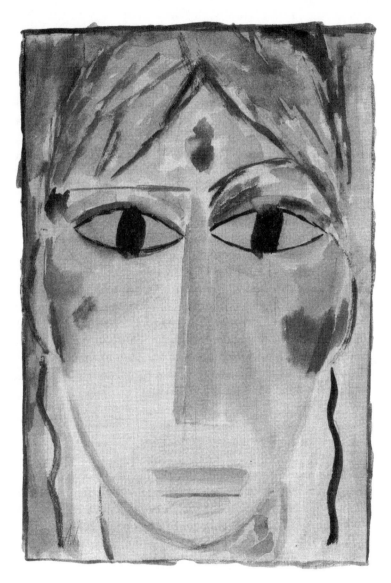

'Countenance of Christ', by Alexey Jawlenski

particular individual in mind. And the look in the eyes belongs to the countenance of Christ. The face of every human being becomes his countenance and becomes a window into the Christ-filled human world.

When art speaks to us the sense world is lifted up into the supersensible realm. When nature speaks to us the supersensible realm becomes perceptible in the world of sense.

Soul life as the language of angels

A person's soul life can also become the language of angels. For example, one morning I thought to myself: Whilst I am visiting an acquaintance in the south of the town this afternoon I could follow that by going to see a young man living in the area who has told me he would like to talk to me sometime. I rang the bell, but nobody answered. Yet I heard noises inside. I went back to my car and waited for a while, wondering what to do, and looking at the street map to find the best way home.

Then someone knocked on my car window. It was the father of the young man I had intended visiting. He was in despair. His wife was trying to commit suicide. He had run to a telephone kiosk to call a doctor, but had been unable to reach one. 'You are sent by heaven,' he said. 'You can surely help us. Our son has not been living with us for a long while now.' He took me into the house and I succeeded in discouraging his depressed wife from ever attempting suicide again. I felt that in giving her this help I had acted as an instrument for her angel. The only thing to my credit was that I had harkened to the call of destiny to visit the son of the sick woman in response to an impulse I could not fully explain.

Feeling as an organ of perception

How are we to distinguish emotions triggered off in the soul by angels from purely human soul emotions? By the fact that the individual in question is not aiming to achieve anything personal. Something is done, usually out of a sudden inspiration, without much examination by thought or reason.

At the time when Russia was still communist and travellers entering the country were put through a thorough examination and their luggage looked through for forbidden articles or things dangerous to the regime, I had in my luggage forbidden literature and religious objects for my Russian friends, i.e. a censer and a picture of the Christ. There were four queues at the customs post. Which one should I join? I saw that every suitcase was being examined to its very bottom, every item taken out. I was dreading the thought that the forbidden items in mine would be discovered. I decided to queue behind a gentleman who looked very good-natured and likeable. When it came to his turn it transpired that he was going to a bear hunt in the Urals. He possessed a number of guns complete with licences and permits. The customs official was so fascinated by these guns that he called to his colleagues to come and look at them. They came, and enjoyed the spectacle tremendously. But so much time was spent on this that he waved the next anxious travellers through the barrier without examining their cases. I felt I was being led by angels. A similar thing happened to a woman who was taking a case full of homeopathic medicines through the customs.

If you are not acting out of self-interest but are taking a risk on behalf of other people, you can be helped if you simply follow your true feeling, and often in the most unusual way. Feeling can become a sense organ for super-sensible promptings, angel guidance, just as many a dream can become a message. Feeling is related to dream consciousness. We can raise it into waking consciousness and it can then tell us something. Through feeling and dreams we can hear and experience not only angels but also people who have died, and elemental beings too.

Conversing in a dream with someone who has passed through death

The girl who died young of whom I spoke in the first chapter conveyed her anxiety in a dream. I dreamt I was sitting on a bench in front of a large cathedral. Inside, a concert had just finished and a lot of young people were streaming out. Two of them broke away from the others and approached me. One of them was this girl I had known well and was fond of, and I did not know the other one. The dead girl began to speak, saying: 'I have a question.' She often used to begin a sentence in that way in life. She then asked: 'What should I do so that the others notice when I want to talk to them?' I did not know what to say. I would so have liked to help the girl, but I did not know the answer myself. Then I woke up and had the feeling the girl was still waiting for my reply. I could sense her presence. In my anxiety at not being able to answer her, I said the Lord's Prayer. The tension relaxed, and within me I heard a gentle 'Thank you', and the feeling of her presence disappeared.

Later on I told the girl's mother about the dream and mentioned the other girl, too, and the dress she was wearing. The mother told me that a short time before her daughter's death her best friend had also died, and this girl used to wear a dress of that description. The two of them had often played music together in an old church, on the organ and a flute. The message conveyed to me by the truth of this dream was that the deceased, especially if they are young, long to remain in touch with the people on earth, and that prayers are of help to them. Not every dream of course is a message from higher worlds. But when this is the case the dreamer is well aware of it.

Messages through dreams

A father whose wife was expecting a baby asked me for an interview. He told me that shortly before waking up from sleep he had had the same dream three times. He dreamt he was in a cathedral and that the name *Ivan* had been repeatedly called down to him from above: *Ivan.* Should he give his child this name? He had been in the war, and at that time German soldiers had called the Russians, their enemy, by that name. I told him that in German Ivan was Johannes, and that in Russian the name was pronounced Iv*an*, i.e. with the stress on the A. Besides, he could add a second name, which could possibly become the name the child was called by. He should have another think about the name given in the dream. His son was born, and in the run-up to the christening the father told me the child was to be called Ivan Sebastian. The father was a musician. When I heard the name I said: 'He will have the name of the great master, Johann Sebastian Bach.' This had not occurred to the father. He beamed with relief, and was very grateful for the guidance. As the boy grew up he was able to identify utterly and wholeheartedly with this name.

A friend of elemental beings

There are people who can actually see elemental beings; not of course with their outer eyes but in an inner imaginative way. You can read about this in the case of people such as Marco Pogacnik.* Other people have a perceptive feeling for hearing those beings speak, or can also experience them silently.

After having had a special experience in the forests of Finland I felt that I, too, was a friend of elemental beings. With a walking companion I had penetrated, without any prescribed route, far into the forest in the Karelia area of northern Finland. I was surprised that we had not heard any birds singing. We came to a clearing which struck us as the kind of place from which great strength emanated. So we made a halt there. Suddenly, as though an invisible conductor had waved his baton, a chorus of birdsong started up. The sound was reinforced by the accompaniment of the wind rustling in the trees like a harpist playing his instrument. This mood was interrupted by the scream of a jay. The bird-song and the soughing of the wind slowly diminished, and the invisible conductor led over to a quieter, more delicate movement of the forest symphony. Then one voice after another joined in, swelling again to a full chorus, and finally fading away slowly. Was this meant to be the answer to my question about songbirds or were we being received in this place where in all probability no human being had ever been before? The Finnish forests are so vast that a few people get lost in them every year. It is also true that in northern Finland Christianity is still very new, and there are still some parts of the natural world which Christian culture has not reached. When the forest

---

*See *Nature Spirits and Elemental Beings* (Findhorn Press 1997).

concert came to an end we waited to see what would happen next. Then it felt to me as though hordes of invisible
beings came crowding round, forest dwellers of earth,
water, air and light, but especially gnomes, the guardians of
the earth, the minerals and the roots. It was as though they
were looking for the element, the sphere of the Christ, the
'Lord of the Elements', as he was called in Celtic Christianity. He had not reached them yet through any human
being. I took out of my bag a small New Testament which I
always carried with me when I was on the move. I opened it
at the third chapter of St John's Gospel, where it says that
the wind bloweth where it listeth. We hear the sound of it
but cannot tell whence it comes nor whither it is going. It is
the conversation Christ has with Nicodemus. I read the
whole chapter aloud. After I had finished we let the echoes
linger for a while. Then my gaze fell on an abundant crop of
wild berries which I had not noticed before. We remained
seated until we heard a quiet murmur of thanks. Then the
sense of a mysterious presence lifted. And the spirits who
had gathered from further afield departed, leaving only
those for whom that glade was home. The berries we
accepted as an offering of thanks.

The first time a feeling perception awoke in me was after I
had been in the Engadine for a few weeks. The gigantic
mountains of primeval rock, covered with everlasting
snow, the blinding white light reminiscent of Greece, the
lake, the babbling brooks and rivers, the intense colours of
the alpine flowers, their aromatic scents and the play of the
clouds, all these things opened me up in soul to new
experiences. I resolved to make a close study of the various
aspects of water. First I looked at the course of a river, and
then at a lake. With the river, constantly new water flows
over the selfsame obstacles. Eddies and currents arise
which are always the same and yet with different water. In

the lake the same stretch of water is there, but the wind blows over it creating different wave forms in the same water. In concentrating on these different states of the water my feeling awoke, and I noticed that in the instances where the wind touched the water, where the water flowed over a stone, round a root or splashed up a bank, and also where the light glistened in the water with silver dapples, in fact wherever two elements encountered one another, it seemed to be 'alive', substantial and ethereal, and with ever-changing moods. There was a continuous arising and disappearing, coming together and dissolving, with serious intention and yet playfulness. I became aware of a new reality which became more and more of a certainty to me, even though I could very seldom speak to anyone about it, for I did not actually 'see' beings. From then on I could exercise this kind of perception in many other areas, though not everywhere, and I also learnt to speak to the beings, and sometimes received a kind of answer.

For instance I was once on a cross-country walk with a friend in torrential rain on a green hill in Ireland. At the top we went our different ways. He wanted to walk further, and I went back to the car. On the way down I discovered that my car key had dropped out of my flapping raincape and must be lying somewhere on the expansive hillside in the lashing storm. I called the young man back to help me look for it, although the situation was obviously hopeless. How was I to find a small key in the heather and the rubble, the grass and the bushes, in the raging wind and rain? My glasses were misted up, so that I could hardly see anything. I left my friend to do the looking and, after the manner of fairytales, I made up a rhyme to the gnomes: 'Direct our gaze, guide our steps,' and repeated it a number of times with great conviction. Suddenly my friend called out: 'I think I've got it!' And there the key actually was, lying on a little slab of stone. In the evening we went back to the place and thanked our invisible helpers. Mutual thanks is always very important if the connection is to continue.

Although elemental beings belong to quite a different sphere from angels, angels can send messages through nature spirits to human beings who are receptive.

Messages via the weather

Elementals are particularly happy to speak to us through the beings active in weather. We notice just how unstable and unpredictable the weather is whenever the weather forecast from the meteorological department does not tally with reality. It is affected by both physical and super-physical influences. If human beings include angels in their sphere of activity these often speak to them through weather phenomena.

This happened to me when I was waiting for a cataract operation. Hanging in my room was a picture of the angel Raphael, the angel of healing, accompanying the young Tobias on his journey. At the angel's bidding he catches a fish with whose liver, heart and kidneys he releases his future wife from a demon and heals his father of his blindness. On the morning of the operation, as soon as I had finished my morning prayer my gaze alighted on this picture. In the otherwise dark room a ray of sunlight fell directly on to the picture and nowhere else. I was surprised, for it was quite impossible for the morning sun to shine into that room. Then I noticed that an open window in the house opposite reflected the sun, and was just the right size to illuminate the picture. I took this to be the angels speaking to me to tell me that my ailing eyes, too, would become seeing again, as had the eyes of the old Tobias. I went through the two operations with complete confidence, and the message came true.

Angels speaking through birds

On another occasion birds were the language medium of angels. A distinguished curative educationalist died unexpectedly whilst on a lecture tour in Germany. He lived in England, but his teaching activity extended throughout the world. He had been present in many places at the founding of new homes for curative education. His name was Alex Baum. He died in December. Outside there was snow, and nature was going through its winter withdrawal. As part of the service for the dead I gave an address. I took the name of the deceased as an image of his being. He had been like a great tree that had spread its branches over all Europe. Many birds had built their nests in this tree and received protection, nourishment, help and understanding there. As I spoke of the tree and the birds, a chorus of birdsong began outside in the garden. At my amen it stopped. The whole of the large congregation had heard it and felt it to be a confirmation of my description of this personality.

Destiny as the language of angels

The more we notice such 'chance' happenings, take them seriously and learn something from them, the more they will come our way as life takes its course. For the angels are dependent on human beings admitting them into their consciousness or into their feelings and actions. Above all they respect human freedom. But apart from this there is a huge area where the speech of angels can be heard, and this is human destiny. Everything could speak to us here, and could be an expression of angels. Particular things sometimes occur simply so that we awaken to this language. Or special things reach through to us precisely because we have practised listening for them. Then 'chance' does not exist for a person any more, and the language of destiny becomes ever clearer. And from the angels' aspect it can more and more become their language.

A Waldorf teacher was talking to a youth group about the course of the year in the botanical gardens. For each month he showed a characteristic slide he had made. For November he showed an example of a certain kind of insect which was hanging on a stalk with its long reddish-coloured legs and very slowly dying. He showed about fifteen pictures to demonstrate how long it takes this insect until it has finally died. All of a sudden the idea shot through me: He is speaking of his own death. Six months later he had a stroke, lost his speech, was paralysed on one side, and lived in this condition for a further seven years. I reminded him of the insect, and he nodded his head vigourously in confirmation.

In another instance destiny spoke in the following way: A twelve-year-old boy was quarrelling with his mother and stormed off angrily on his bike. Shortly afterwards his mother heard him calling up to her from the road, and she opened the window. He waved to her and said an affectionate 'good-bye'. A few minutes later he had an accident with his bike and did not regain consciousness. Ten days later he died.

The language of destiny can be active not only with regard to death but also in and for life. Over many years I narrated fairytales and stories at public venues. Among these were stories about the stars as gates or portals. For example the twelve apostles each entered through one of these starry gates with a particular impulse in keeping with the nature of that gate. Many years later a young man came and told me he had heard the 'Taurus' story, and had not dared ask any further questions because his friend thought it was all nonsense. But the memory of the story had stayed with him ever since. He wanted to talk to me about how he could bring this impulse to realization in life, for he was born in the sign of Taurus. He is now a medical doctor practising the contributions Rudolf Steiner has made to the art of healing, and he has also brought them to countries in the East.

What are angels telling us through misfortune and pain?

The most difficult thing for us human beings is that pain and misfortune also want to tell us something. If we learn to understand this language we can subsequently gain something from any situation in a way that brings us closer both to ourself and to the worlds of the angels. Those who do not want to learn anything from painful situations will have to suffer them over and over again. They are then aware of being buffeted by destiny yet do not notice that they themselves keep hitting back at it. Leo Tolstoi's narrative 'The Godson' tells of the godson coming upon a bear trap in the forest. A heavy log of wood has been tied above a pot of honey. Along comes a bear with her cubs. The log of wood bothers her and she pushes it away with her paw. It swings back and kills one of the cubs. In great anger the mother bear pushes the log of wood away from the honey pot again and another one of the cubs is then killed. This happens again and again until the log finally kills her too.

Human beings have to learn to see the serious threats

connected with the sweet things in life as part of the picture, and not to push them away aggressively in annoyance and anger. How many marriages and partnerships have the intention of being beneficial. Then one day the threat is discovered, namely the karma which has to be coped with, but in a way that enables it not to do harm but to encourage new capacities to develop in one another and for one another.

There was a marriage which got into great difficulties. The husband became the victim of an incurable illness. The couple were told that he only had a few more years to live. They made an entirely new approach to their life together and made a biographical work of art of the last years of his life. As far as he had the strength for it they read books on themes of existential importance and discussed them, listened to music, looked at pictures and studied nature. They did all this so as to cultivate a love for earthly things which would reach beyond death. In the doing of all this their love for one another was renewed. And this enabled the wife to undertake, out of love, the heavy task of caring for her husband during his last days.

In the case of another marriage a third person had intruded. The wife had always kept a fearful and jealous eye on her husband for fear of losing him. Nevertheless they were heading for divorce. She was in despair. Her feelings increasingly got the better of her, so that she became more and more unbearable to her husband. So I drew her attention to whether she might not ask herself what this might be telling her. This thought had never occurred to her. So she began to converse with me about it. She discovered that she had wanted to possess her husband as though he were her property. So he had freed himself from this cage. She made the discovery that you have many kinds of relationships with other people and that you will of course have encountered many of them in past lives. There are karmic tasks to tackle. Yet she had a real feeling that over the years of their marriage a quite individual, unique bond had arisen between herself and her husband, the spirit of their partnership. Thoughts such as these calmed her troubled feelings. She wrote these all down, with the possibility of showing this to him one day. She tried every day both to let go of the inner hold on him and to connect herself more with this objective spirit of their marriage, which she was very aware of even when her husband was not with her, and which had woven a karmic link between them which continued to work in some way because it had not yet come to an end. In fact she acquired confidence in her marriage angel who no doubt wanted to lead her through this difficult time to new inner experiences.

What I told her husband was that the reason why most marriages break down is because the people are not prepared to go through processes of change. A marriage has to be able to go through a death process, for only then will there be development and resurrection. Accept death, but not out of escapism but out of faith in your togetherness. To start with the husband did not know what to make of this advice. His new relationship was so rewarding and easy. Yet after a while a crisis came about there, too. He had already met with a number of similar problems in the course of his marriage. They now returned in a changed form. What was this telling him? Should he learn to come to terms with a death process as I had advised? All of a sudden he saw his wife, in her inner being, as he had seen her while he was still in love with her. That was something that was not subject to death. He felt this love anew. He went and told her about it and she told him what she had meanwhile been experiencing and had written down. Then they realized that through the death of their marriage they had been helped to experience its resurrection. They both accepted seriously that their partnership had its angel. The wife had overcome jealousy and possessiveness. The husband gave the other relationship another form. The two ladies became friends, and with hindsight the crisis became for all three of them a clear message from their angels.

The death of a person you love, even of someone young whose departure leaves a deep gap behind, needs to be understood as a message. A young woman, a painter and photographer, gave birth to her first child. Ten days later she came down with terrible convulsions and was in a life-threatening state. The medical superintendent at the clinic was at his wits' end. He summoned a council of specialists of the highest level. They were unable to find the cause of the trouble. The woman died. They did a post mortem and discovered that the cause was intestinal obstruction. This occurs very often after giving birth, and it can be put right by an immediate operation. The group of specialists had not hit on the obvious explanation. They themselves were baffled about how stuck they had been. The parents of the young woman refrained from blaming them, for they could see from the artistic work left behind by their daughter that this had reached a completion and that her life had come to a close. The child flourished with its father and later on with a new mother. Everyone concerned accepted the language of destiny.

Between you and me

Demons and angels in our conversations

We have been considering an angel of a community who is active between people, i.e. a marriage angel. This angel remains connected with this communal bond for a long time, through ups and downs, as long as the bond exists. In fact every time there is an intense involvement between people, even if this is short-lived and temporary, a spiritual being is active between them, a light or a dark one. A dark one brings people under compulsion, and a light one enables them to grow beyond themselves. We are all familiar with the way we always tend to fall into the same pattern in the way we react to someone we meet. There are provocative phrases that cause the other person to react violently. Instead of avoiding such a phrase, or on the other hand intentionally remaining calm for once, it slips out to our own annoyance, and the other reacts in the usual way. These are real demons of compulsion which are difficult to get rid of. The best thing to do is actually to recognize them as such, become conscious of their compelling power that often follows us into the night and disturbs our sleep. A situation of this kind arouses agitated thoughts and feelings, anger, annoyance and helplessness. These spin round in repetitive circles. The only thing that will help will be an understanding of the situation. Something has taken an independent form between the two people and now exercises its power over them. Not until you yourself confine it in a definite form will it leave you in peace.

The best thing to do when you are under this kind of

torment is to get up in the night, when such torment is at its worst, and write down in proper sequence what has otherwise been going through your mind in the form of confused thoughts and feelings. In writing it down it can even happen that you see quite new and positive ways of tackling the situation. You see aspects of the other person's character to which your emotions had previously blinded you. It is as though a heavy load or strain had been lifted. You have the feeling of having achieved something, of having fought a battle, and having raised what lay between you on to a higher level from where you can see things from a higher vantage point. Now you can go to sleep. You can meet the other person without hidden rejection and aggression. This has been made possible through your own activity. You have placed outside yourself the reason why your thoughts and feelings were going round in circles, you have set them in order by writing them down.

This can also happen by having a conscious and honest conversation. If it is still possible, a helping being can insert itself into the soul endeavours. A spirit of reconciliation can then replace the being that brought the compulsion. This can only happen where an effort is being made in a struggling soul. These beings work in many different ways in everything going on in the 'in between' realm. This can be between human beings. It can also be in the creating or experiencing of art or ritual, or in applying oneself with devotion to a being in nature. A real conversation, whether between two people or among a group of people, is shared by an angel living among the participants and clothing itself in the words being exchanged. This can be seen in the fact that not only does the one person take up the thoughts of another, bring movement into them and possibly make them his or her own, but also in that all the participants are enabled to have thoughts, experiences and emotions they have never had before. One of them says it, but it feels to the others as though they said it themselves. After a conversation of this kind they all feel exhilarated, lifted into the sphere of community. And what they received from this is not wasted but works its way into everyday life.

A young woman described how she had transformed into action something that originated in a conversation of this kind. She was walking through a long underground railway subway and was being harrassed by a man. Despite her discouragements he would not go away. She still had a further distance to go along empty streets. Then she remembered being part of a conversation of this sort where the theme had been the power of the word, and that if it comes forth from the centre of one's own being and not out of fear it drives evil powers away, as Jesus did who said to the tempter: 'Get thee gone.' So she looked the man straight in the eyes – this man who in this situation was acting as an instrument of evil – and said loudly and clearly: 'Go away.' At which he turned and fled.

Angels speaking when human beings remain silent

Remaining silent can also be a form of conversation in which a being of destiny is experienced between the people who are maintaining a silence.

I became ill whilst away on holiday. I could not continue my journey as planned to the place where I wanted to stay. The doctor was called. He came every day to get rid of the temperature of which he could not find the cause. It was in a country in which people still found time for one another. Although the two of us belonged to different nationalities and English was not our mother tongue, so that an understanding by way of language was very limited, conversations arose in the language of the heart. On the last of the doctor's visits we remained silent for a long while, and into this silence there came a being which blessed our meeting. The next day I was well enough to continue my journey. The purpose of the illness had been fulfilled.

Invisible sculpture

For his performances known as 'actions', the controversial artist Joseph Beuys coined the concept 'social sculpture'. He wanted the installations he created to stimulate people to come into conversation, into a communal search for meaning, a togetherness. For him, the actual work of art was not the 'Honey Pump' or the 'Blob of Fat' but what arose between people because of these, also between him and the viewers of the exhibition. He and the viewers produced, at the instigation of what was visible, an invisible sculpture, namely what was formed invisibly among them. At the Lenbach Gallery in Munich you can see a room that was arranged by Beuys originally for 'Documenta 6' in Kassel, the large international art show. He was a part of this work. Each day of the exhibition he created a new social sculpture together with the viewers. Beuys is no longer alive today, and we can wonder what significance this couch, this medicine chest, these implements on the wall, this dusty inventory of the room might have without him being there. Beuys gave it the name 'Show your Wound'. I visited this room with a friend. I asked him whether he could make anything of it. His answer was: 'Just as the Christ once upon a time showed his wound to doubting Thomas, thus curing him of doubt, nowadays he says to us: "Show your wound," for only then can you be helped, only then can you experience me as a healer.' The actual conversation brought about between the two of them through Beuys was social sculpture. People are part of it. Without them the props remain so many unused objects.

I continued to occupy myself with the question of invisible sculpture. I took part in the Act of Consecration of Man* as it is celebrated in the Christian Community. And during a service I experienced quite clearly and consciously that the visible parts of it, the altar, candles, the picture, the chalice, the priest through word and gesture, and the congregation too, are a kind of sounding-board for what is occurring in between them all. The essential being of it all, i.e. the being of the occurrence, is what takes place invisibly between the visible parts. An invisible sculpture arises into which a spiritual being can enter and be active. I was very moved by this experience and described it to the priest who celebrated the service. He was profoundly affected by what I told him, for throughout the service he had felt the presence of Joseph Beuys without understanding why.

What has come particularly clearly to people's notice through Beuys and his work is actually true in the case of every genuine work of art. What classifies a work of art as the real thing is not because of it being particularly true to nature or especially 'beautiful', or because it gives a particularly good portrayal of something seen with the inner eye, but that something is going on between the figures and colours, the forms and the beings depicted there, which means that something is also going on between the viewers and the creation as such. There are pictures which seem very promising at first sight, and beautiful to look at. Yet after a little while there is no longer any movement between the viewers and the picture. It does not live in them but remains always the same, no longer speaking to them anew

---

* The communion service of the Christian Community Church.

in the present, in the here and now. Other pictures become accessible less quickly. You have to open yourself to them and let them in, until you have discovered the secret hidden in the visible part. Paul Klee said: 'Art makes the invisible visible.' Today we can add: 'Between the visible parts the invisible realm appears to the soul.' Or: 'The invisible element appears in the spaces between the visible elements.' This so-called new concept of art can also be applied to old art, assuming that the viewer really takes the time to look, and is not satisfied merely to know the title of the picture and the name of the artist. If you grasp this, then pictures can become things you live with, and with which you are always having fresh conversations.

The same of course holds good for works of poetry and music. Do we not find that we love them more and more deeply the more often we hear them?

Experiencing the 'in-between' in nature

We human beings can have a different kind of 'in-between experience' in nature. Here it is often the reverse of the way it is with art. We arrive at some particular place in nature and are immediately struck by an experience that is new to us.

I went to Ireland on holiday. As soon as I could be alone with nature, wherever it happened to be, I felt at home in a way I felt about nowhere else in the world. The essence of the Irish landscape gave me a feeling that was home to my soul, a feeling of expanse and of life between heaven and earth, between all the elements, between clouds, light, wind, surging sea and the colours of the earth: green, grey-violet, golden yellow. Then, for the first time, I saw the rocky crowns of the Skellig Michael Islands towering up out of the sea. They seemed to be a greeting to me from the angel of this landscape. On the one island live thousands of birds of all kinds. On the other one, over a thousand years ago monks built a small monastery with stone cells like beehives, a little cemetery and a simple cross in human form sculptured out of slate. These were dedicated to Michael who is the spirit of our present age. Yet when I first saw them I did not realize this. I just felt called upon to meet the spirituality of this land in the same way one can meet a person. The more often I did this—from then on I went there many times—the more strongly I experienced that, contrary to my initial assumption, it was not primordial spirituality speaking to me from Celtic Christianity but something of the future, that a being of Michaelic spirituality was inspiring me. This was what started me writing, first for children and then for adults. Thoughts and words came to me from a thoroughly modern spirituality, belonging as much to the earth as to the cosmos, as much to humankind as a whole as to each individual human being.

However, what human beings experience between themselves and nature can be much more delicate, much more 'natural'. I discovered very late in life that I had best friends of a visible-invisible kind very near my home. I had known of course for a long time that my town in Germany had an 'English Garden' many kilometres long. But I had never taken the time to give it my attention. I had once taken a walk there and also been there with visitors with whom I talked about all sorts of things without really taking notice of my natural surroundings. One day I went there by myself. And it struck me as though a particular tree spoke to me. It was late autumn and the tree had already shed its leaves. It looked at me through two great swellings in its bark. I stood still and admired the bare branches growing like antlers from the trunk that had a face. I let the being of the tree work on me for a long time. Then suddenly—but for only a passing moment—a surge of love flowed between me and the tree. This was the start of a new association with the beings who want to make themselves noticed invisibly in this realm between visible nature and human beings. From then on I went as often as I possibly could to the English Garden. More and more of the trees spoke to me. They accompanied me through the course of the year, through all the changes from bare branches to the delicate buds which put forth their tiny leaves of light-filled green, from the splendour of the leaves of summer to their gold and red in autumn until they turn brown and carpet the earth. The tree through which I awoke to this was an English elm with heart-shaped leaves. Whenever I came near it it seemed to me as though it was already calling to me, welcoming me with joy, and hoping for a conversation. I would then tell it about all the changes I saw it had passed through, how I rejoiced over them and how much I admired it.

On one occasion I walked right past it, lost in thought. Then it came over me that someone was calling. I turned round and saw that I had walked past my tree friend without greeting it or even noticing it. So I turned back and made this good. There was joy between us. In fact it was not only trees and the small meadow flowers or bushes which formed a connection with me but each area of this wild parkland has something like its own spirit. There are various groups of trees which seem to have the choreography of a dance. There are meadows surrounded by bushes and trees which, as self-contained structures, have a soul of their own. Anyone who wants to experience this must be able to keep still and, whilst looking with outer sight, listen inwardly and create a connection to this piece of earth. If you do this very often you will be able to confirm the experience Hans Müller-Wiedemann expressed in a poem:

> Practising Love
>
> Walk the one path many a time
> Not for knowing but for greeting
> the tree at the corner,
> for becoming familiar
> with the grassy valley
> and also the clearing
> that again and again
> lets in the sky.
> Walk the path many a time
> until it is yours.
> You are practising love.

This is the way that, in all spheres of life, we human beings can find spirituality between outer things and include them in our own life.

Breathing spaces

Disregard of breathing spaces in the course of history

A breathing space is closely related to what we have described as an in-between realm. And yet the two are different. Anton Bruckner is a master of the musical breathing space — the rest. The rests in his symphonies give the hearer a chance to hear the ending. As with someone's death there is an after-echo of the life lived and then a continuation of life on a higher level. With Bruckner the music often rises in waves, higher and higher, opening up the heavens more and more in the direction of a resurrection. Every rest has a little death hidden in it from which that which has reached a conclusion can arise anew. In any piece of music there is an activity at work amongst all that is audible to the senses, in fact this is what the music is. Music lives in the intervals between the notes, between the chords, in the rhythm which arises out of a whole number of tiny in-between spaces, whereas the rests are the void out of which a new content will be born. They are the matrix for what is going to spring forth out of what has passed away.

Life has similar breathing spaces. These are important if time is not to become a 'pastime', where one kills time, has no time, is short of time. The ancient expression: 'The time has come,' does not only mean that the moment has arrived for a certain event to happen, e.g. the birth of Jesus, but also that the waiting time is over. When an event occurs it fulfils the promise of a longer or shorter period preceding it. There are breathing spaces in history too, where that which has been has to die away to let the new element in. At the present moment the German people are living in this kind of breathing space in their history. Yet most people think of this interval as a time they do not want to lose out on. 'Lose no time,' for 'time is money'. This kind of attitude throttles a breathing space. The century is drawing to its conclusion with all the positive and negative events that have happened in this nation. It is not a matter of simply carrying on as though none of these had happened. There should be a pause for listening to the resonances of both the new impulses that can lead to the healing of the earth and mankind and to the resonances of the catastrophe of the holocaust. Instead of this, the positive element is frequently swallowed up by disputing and compromising with the dark forces, and the dark side is repressed. Whether it is a political party or a college of teachers, a business council or a religious community, they foregather to realize new plans for salvation and enlightenment. Then they begin to fall out. People cannot agree. But nor can they respect the others for what they are. Their togetherness is weakened by the dark forces in their own being which they refuse to see. Then they make compromises with the world's dark forces which they originally wanted to oppose with their ideals of human dignity, faith in the spirit and hope in the future. The German people have not wanted to allow time for a breathing space in which alongside external rehabilitation an inner change of attitude, a new cultural impulse could have arisen among the ruins of civilization. Only in the instances where Germany's dark era is recognized to its full extent, from the roots of the evil to its present-day consequences, and calls forth a corresponding pain which, if felt deeply enough, becomes birth pangs, can the real spirit of Central Europe return to the national organism.

There is also something else which belongs here. Those healing impulses which, through the inclusion of the supersensible element in education, medicine, agriculture, religion, judicial and economic life have begun to work in our time, must not be permitted to be eclipsed or distorted into rigid rules and laws by the sheer force of intellect and emotion. In the first third of the twentieth century not only in Germany but in Central Europe as a whole, positive forces began to appear and there were reform movements in all areas of education, sociology, art, endeavours towards democracy, and much more. In the second third of the century the dark forces reared their heads and made themselves felt over the whole of Europe even as far as America and Asia and back again to Germany. In the last third of the century people, especially the young, began to awaken to a realization of what had happened, both the light aspect and the dark.

Other members of this generation imagined they would find access to the spiritual world through drugs. They did not allow a breathing space either, and filled time with illusions, ecstasy and self-satisfaction.

Others again picked up the impulses where they had left them in the 1930s. Huge enthusiasm, dedicated sacrifice, the will to rebuild lived in all this, but these people, too, did not allow for a breathing space in which to hear the echoes of all that had been.

Instead of a breathing space, what occurred in all areas was a splitting up, like a demonic counter-image of a space in which to breathe. This separating, disunion, dissention has become symptomatic of present-day humankind: atomic fission, the splitting of consciousness, the split between East and West, North and South, dissention even among the ranks of like-minded people, the split between morality and politics — which was described publicly in a TV interview by an influential politician in the words: 'Politics has nothing to do with morality.'

Making room for an unexpected breathing space

I once asked a class 10 the question as to where we can see evidence of the presence of Christ. An intense silence ensued. The pupils and I let it continue. Each one of them thought about it in his or her own way, or noticed the silence, which began as an emptiness in which nobody knew what to say, but which went through a noticeable change. Then one of the girls said: 'It was like that just now.' And a boy added: 'Now that you've said so, it's over.'

A space which is filled with such a pregnant experience is of course rare. It cannot be induced. It is a gift. Our part in it is to receive it in the sense of a saying by Friedrich Doldinger: 'Pay attention to the spaces, however small, which destiny brings you. Some day the One who is to come will come this way.'

The power of peace

At the end of the twentieth century there were many peace movements. The people belonging to them made room for the positive and negative happenings of the past century to re-echo in them and for the essence of the future to announce itself soundlessly, as it does during a rest in a Bruckner symphony. But these peaceful interludes were also full of powerlessness. They survived the powerlessness by using it as a space for breathing, with their non-violence and their trust in the power of peace.

There was a family flying to Israel with their three small children. I was struck by how peaceful and content the children were throughout the flight. While we were showing our passports I got into conversation with their parents. They were on their way to Jerusalem to pray, together with others, for peace. They had done the same thing in Hiroshima, at the Berlin Wall, and other centres of dissension. But this could have an effect only if peace was consciously cultivated in their own family and also in their place of work and in their circle of friends. The important thing on each occasion was to make room for a space so as to hear what significance the past had and to gain the strength to meet with trust what was coming in the future. These people, both individually and also as a peace movement, open gates to let angels in. The miracle of the fall of the Wall could happen despite the fact that hardly anyone had believed it possible any more. And it happened through the power of non-violence, though there were a few smart commentators who afterwards said they had seen it coming. Communism had come to an end both in politics and in economics. It became possible through co-operation between human beings and angels who wanted to serve each other in the interest of peace on earth. And the meeting, which for most of those people was unconscious, took place in the breathing space for which they consciously made room. Yet in the destiny of the now re-united German people and of all the other people in liberated Eastern Europe, a breathing space is no longer permitted. Capitalism seized hold of the nations and brought chaos upon them. It was exactly the same with spiritual movements. They flooded into the eastern nations who had no power of discrimination. Even the therapeutic impulses in education and many other areas of life were taken up without pause, much too fast, and without going into the depths or being inwardly digested. The Wall is not there externally today. But the dissension between East and West, rich and poor, politics and morality is greater than ever.

The enemy of the breathing space

The enemy of intervals in time has invented offers for passing the time which either titillate or fill people with boredom. Not until people make room again for breathing spaces in their lives as individuals, as communities, as nations, will individuals and nations come to themselves, to their spiritual core; and this spiritual substance, this angelic substance can resolve all dissension in the organism to which it belongs. Turning our gaze backwards to the past century and forwards to the coming century challenges us to pause and take breath, so that the things that have happened can re-echo and the hope of the future can declare itself.

'It was time, not me'

Someone once had a totally different experience of an interval in time as something containing potential change. In the 1930s Friedrich Doldinger made a picture, a silk inlay, representing the Christ. Most people who saw the picture were horrified. There were very few who could accept it. Decades later, when the Third Reich had been over in Germany for a long time, there was an exhibition of his pictures. He visited the exhibition with an old friend. When this friend saw the picture of the Christ he was quite taken aback. He knew the picture from before. He stood there and looked at it for a long time, and then said to Doldinger: 'Well, what a lot of work you have put into that one!' To which Doldinger replied: 'It was not me but time.' He had not added a single brush stroke to it. So his friend came to realize that during the interval in which he had not seen the picture the events going on all around them had turned this picture from something which was past into something indicative of the future. Externally it came from the past but in its inner gesture it spoke of the future. The viewer was touched by the presence of the spirit living in every acknowledged interval. One cannot of course in a logical sense reckon the whole of the intervening time as an interval. Something was happening all the time. But in the way Doldinger's friend experienced the picture there had been an interval.

Similarly, the time we live in is, logically, also not an interval. It is constantly being filled with events and developments. But where the activity of the Central European folk spirit is concerned it is an interval. We are living between the time at the beginning of the twentieth century when it ceased to be a force for good, and the time when it will be reborn in the future, after the consequences of the catastrophes of that century have been taken to heart. The deadly occurrences in the middle of the century were like an explosion blasting the activity of the folk spirit to smithereens. Not until we become conscious of the noise of the explosion and the consequences it had can the folk spirit approach us from the future. We must let there be an interval in the drama in order to enable the change to come about out of our silence and our loss, and out of the gaping abyss of evil which it opened up.

Meditation as a breathing space in everyday life

If we are to understand and be able to make use of intervals occurring in large, historical connections that are way beyond anything personal, we need to have intervals or breathing spaces in our own personal lives. These spaces give us the chance to lift ourselves above earthly time and enter a world of timelessness, which is the world of the spirit, of spiritual beings, of angels. Every meditation, prayer or sacrament is a space of this kind if we enter into it in a way which makes us forget time. As long as I think: 'How much longer shall I continue?' or: 'I have no more time, my work is calling me,' I have not allowed a real space to exist but have remained in earthly time. When meditation becomes a space in everyday existence a moment can have the quality of eternity, eternity flashes up in the instant. Such experiences are difficult to describe because the kind of concepts we use on earth do not quite correspond to them. A single word can become a world. When we put ourselves into a mood which is that of a breathing space, i.e. when we empty ourselves of all wilfulness, of all our habitual thinking and willing and are ready to receive what wants to come, then even single words can transport us to timelessness, into a world beyond time, which is eternity.

We have the word 'existence'. If you give yourself up to experiencing it all around you you feel in a state of inner quiet. Existence is something which supports you, it is dependable, without a beginning or an end, and can be experienced in everything that has been created. We can feel we have ground under our feet. We are secure, protected. And then, all of a sudden, in the midst of our experience of breadth, depth and expansiveness, 'existence' can be experienced quite differently, in the sense of our having an individual existence, existing in the present, at this precise moment. When these two opposite experiences of 'existence' melt into one a person experiences eternity in the moment as light and a moment of eternity as force. This is a real interval after and before the experiences of everyday life.

I experienced one of these intervals before I left home to

go to work one morning. Then I took part in a group discussion which continued later in a smaller circle. At this point my colleagues complained that I had been talking about things that did not concern other people, and that I had been indiscreet. This hit me hard, for I felt they were right. I went home at lunchtime very upset. Still filled with horror at myself I suddenly continued the interval experience of the morning. I was lifted out of time and 'saw' — i.e. perceived with my inner eye — that everything is part of one huge whole. My trusting nature can assume the character of indiscretion, yet at the same time it is the openness which people appreciate in me and which they can trust in. And far beyond the scope of this actual situation I saw the world as a huge entity complete in itself, with all its light aspects and its dark aspects, all its contrasts being part of it; and it was really indescribable. I was overcome with joy at this experience. I felt it was an experience of enlightenment coming to me in the middle of everyday life from out of my morning breathing space.

Nevertheless you should take care not to combine meditation and prayer with an intent to achieve something in particular, to cultivate them so that something definite will happen. A lack of wilfulness is of the essence in such intervals.

In his book *Zen in the Art of Archery* Eugen Herrigel relates that it took him five years of practice until he had overcome wilfulness to the point where he could hit the bull's-eye without aiming. His teacher could do it blindfold. At the second shot the arrow split the first which was still sticking in the bull's-eye. Unintentionality is the letting go of wilfulness. In these gaps between the otherwise intentional actions of earthly life the angel can enter in — the angels of individuals or of the community — or even the Christ whom angels and human beings serve in common.

Powerlessness

Help from out of the night

We have already described experiences of powerlessness in the chapter on identity, especially in the realm of education. I should like to add a few things from this new aspect.

In a class, one of the boys wanted to keep on provoking me by putting his feet on the desk during the lesson. I told him to take them off the desk, but he soon put them back up again. For a while I let him have his way, but his attitude upset me considerably. In a stern voice I told him once more to stop it. I knew that he wanted to drive this game to a head so that he would infuriate me and I would throw him out of the lesson. I did not want to give him that satisfaction. But I felt powerless to deal with him. The evening before the next lesson I thought for a long time about what I ought to do with the boy; ignore his behaviour or take action? What was the cause of the power struggle? I asked myself this sort of question as I thought about the inner nature of the boy, but this did not at all lessen my powerlessness. Next day I went to the lesson with dread. What happened? I was filled with amazement, for without my having said anything he did not once put his feet on the desk, nor did he do so ever again. While I was going through a feeling of helplessness and trying to feel my way to the being of the boy I must have reached his angel, his higher being, and this brought him into harmony with himself. In my powerlessness his angel became strong, as Paul says in the words: 'For in weak people God is strong.'

'If that isn't the last straw!'

Every mother and father knows these feelings of powerlessness in dealing with young sons and daughters. If you
do not try to keep such feelings at bay but admit them you
will receive help together with unexpected insight into
destiny.

A girl had run away from a home for drug-damaged
young people. The therapist responsible for her set out to
look for her and found her on the road a few kilometres
from the home. He tried to get her to change her mind and
go back with him, but she was in no way ready to do so. All
his educational and therapeutic skills left him at his wits'
end. Then in the distance he saw the milkfloat being driven
by a woman who weighed a ton and was totally unkempt
and degenerate. He knew her, and he thought to himself: 'If
that isn't the last straw!' The positive side of this situation
was about to dawn on him for the first time in its full significance. The woman braked, got out looking like some
monster, stammered something and then drove off again.
The girl was deeply moved by this scene and whispered:
'She is much more of a wreck even than I am,' and was then
ready to return to the home. The therapist gave silent
thanks to the invisible helpers who had so arranged things
that the person whose arrival he took to be the last straw
came along just at the moment of his powerlessness.

Some readers are likely to say, 'I have often been in such
situations of inner powerlessness, but I have never received
help like that.' This can be due to various reasons which are
actually covered in the above description, namely that we
must have learnt to be accountable even when powerless.
We have to learn to notice what things and processes are
trying to tell us. We must not think that a certain way of
behaving or the doing of a particular exercise will call in the

help of higher powers, but we must realize that it belongs to our destiny and our level of development if nothing of the sort happens. But if it nevertheless happens, it is not our merit but a gift, a grace for which we feel very grateful. Not until we stop seeing strokes of fate or angelic guidance as chance happenings but take them seriously, can the beings standing behind them become clearly felt in our lives. We must put this attitude into practice, and also practise paying attention to processes going on in between things — to breathing spaces — whilst at the same time taking nothing for granted. This is not an easy condition to achieve, yet it is possible for everyone to do it.

Experiencing Christ in powerlessness

Whilst going through a very profound and painful experience of powerlessness I was granted an unusual form of comfort which can also be of comfort to other people who do not have this same experience. I was suffering indescribably under the burden of not being able to prevent someone I loved from doing something wrong which would also do great harm to himself. He presented a completely deaf ear to my concerns, warnings and prophesies. He closed himself off entirely to what would have been for his good. Not to be able to protect a loved one from disaster must be one of the most difficult experiences of powerlessness. In this predicament I prayed for my friend. And I felt as though someone else was speaking to me in my thoughts. 'What you are now experiencing with this particular human being is something that I experience with an infinite number of human beings daily. I love them and want to shield them from disaster, but they will not let me near them. For the sake of their freedom I suffer power-

lessness every day. Your experience of powerlessness con-
nects you with me and brings you close to me. I am with
you always. You can now feel this, thanks to your powerlessness. Thank him who lives in your powerlessness.'

This was an experience of powerlessness which helped
me to see with new eyes for the rest of my life. Two thousand years ago the Christ became connected with earthly
human beings for all time. He lives, suffers and rejoices in
everything that human beings experience, suffer and rejoice
over. He is 'the human being' in every human being, as
Pilate prophesied when he pointed to him and said: 'Ecce
homo,' behold the human being.

Being a creative person

Being creative is an artistic activity

To be capable of creativity is a part of being human. Being creative is not the same as being busy. We can be busy all day, but we will not always have produced something creative. Even if we have made a technological discovery we use the word 'construct' or 'invent' and do not say we have created a new computer or new method of execution. Creating is working with living things, changing and transforming them, bringing movement into them. Creating is always an artistic process, even if it occurs entirely in the everyday sphere. A woman can manage to get the family's dinner on the table on time. She can also create a meal whose very appearance is part of the nourishment, and the very taste tells you that it was cooked with love. We actually distinguish between cooking and cooking-as-an-art, and this does not depend on the number of ingredients used. Creating of any kind can be called art: the art of education, the art of medicine, of sociology and gardening, and the art of life. For this kind of creative activity contains the essence of art, which is to include death in life. What is created by these means may die without being grieved over, for with further creative effort it will live on in such a way that it changes something in the creator, awakening in him or her a new perception and a new understanding.

When we write a book we put our own soul, our own life into it. It dies at the stage of the black, printed letters, but it can be brought to life again when it is read by people who do not merely string one sentence to another but create the content anew in that it opens their eyes to a new way of looking at things or confirms their own view. This happens with every art form — music, painting, and also with every example of the art of life.

The art of life in the classroom

Another characteristic of creating is the way producing and receiving interrelate. In nature this happens by way of male and female, i.e. through two different entities. In the realm of soul and spirit the male and female can be in one person. All artists are producers, and in the course of presenting what they have produced they are also receivers. This applies equally well to the arts of life. Teachers have a lot to do to prepare their lessons. If a lesson is also to be a work of art they have to be prepared to receive what comes to them either from the pupils or from the spirit of the situation. If they bring only what they have prepared, they may, by the end of the lesson, have 'done' the subject matter, and perhaps they themselves are also 'done in', but they will not have done the lesson full justice, will not have let life enter in, nor death out of which new life arises.

I had prepared myself to tell the children of a class 3 the story of Esther from the Old Testament. When I entered the classroom I found the chairs lined up two and two in the gangway between the desks. The children were standing against the walls, waiting expectantly to see what I would do. The so-called normal thing to have done would probably have been to tell the children to put the chairs and themselves back in their right places. I felt the tension in the air, and I said: 'Oh, so you want to travel by train today. Get in then.' I proceeded to distribute the roles: ticket collector, passengers, stationmaster and driver. They all said where they wanted to travel to on the stretch between Munich and Copenhagen. On the way, the train began to go slower and slower. Eventually the driver announced that the engine was faulty and would have to stop before it reached a station. It would take a while before the engine could be exchanged for another. The religion teacher happened to be among the passengers. She offered to tell the waiting passengers a story. They happily agreed, and sat down on the green meadow, i.e. the floor of the classroom. Then the stationmaster came up to me and told me very shyly that he would love to hear the story, but as stationmaster he was as far away as the station. I told him he should come over from the station with an engine to see what was wrong with the train. He did so, and in this splendid setting we had the story of Esther.

The art of life in dealing with teenagers

Being creative with teenagers is to be ready to have a real conversation. In a circle of young people Christianity and Communism were being heatedly discussed. Finally I said: 'I would now like to summarize in an absolutely objective way what has transpired in this conversation.' I described the statements and opinions of both sides from what I thought was an objective angle. When I had finished, one of the boys said: 'Fine, but it was possible to hear quite clearly which side you are on.' I could see his point, and the young people let it stand. Did they sense that it is more in keeping with the spirit of the hour to pay attention to the thoughts of those who think differently from you while at the same time remaining true to yourself, rather than merely putting on a show of agreeing with them?

The art of life in a partnership

This kind of presence of mind is necessary for any real creativity. Even a doctor has first of all to carry out a thorough examination, but then be prepared to receive an intuition which departs entirely from the usual approach. And when people go to a marriage or family counsellor in order to be creative in the art of life, they may accept all the advice given to them based on either experience or rules. Their lives will nevertheless only become a work of art if they make way for the spirit of the hour which, rather than telling them where the difficulties originate, tells them that they can create something new out of them.

A couple who had been living together for quite a long time wanted to get married. While they were on the way to a meeting to prepare themselves for marriage they broke into a loud quarrel as they came up the stairs. I asked them whether they did not want to allow themselves more time to examine their resolve to get married. The quarrel was not exactly a good omen. To which they both said that they realized they would constantly have to go through such quarrels, and that it was a task of their common destiny. They were learning to cope with this better and better, but they should not suppress it. Each time it happened it helped them both to come to themselves and they could then live together again. The conversation among the three of us turned into a real preparatory meeting, different from the way I had prepared it, but filled with the spirit of the present moment. They left the building hand in hand. The marriage has been intact now for almost twenty years. But beware of making a hard and fast rule of this. How many people have made the secret confession that on their way to the Register Office they would far rather have turned back!

Material for the creator in us

There is nothing that cannot be lifted into the sphere of creativity. Even our dealings with illness, misfortune or loss can be material for our creativity. We can recognize true creativity if it is a case of having accepted the situation as given and then making way for ideas that give it a new form. We do not appear to be responsible for the given situation, yet we can make it our own. Ideas also come from somewhere or other. This often only occurs to us when we begin to give positive acceptance to the given situation. We then become the place where the connection comes about between what destiny brings and the new impulse that occurs to us. We do the creating, though it is actually the beings behind both destiny and the ideas who are being active in the ideas we have. All genuine artists experience something intangible existing in their own creativity, which is as intangible and yet as real as a divine being, even if they do not call it that.

Love

Love purifies

There is no human love in which the love of Christ does not
live, for he does not love one thing but not another. He
himself is the Being of Love. Love is a being and this being
is the Christ. Christ also lives in everything human beings
experience. When human beings suffer hatred, degradation
and ill-treatment then the Being of Love suffers in them —
Christ suffers, the real human being suffers in every human
imperfection. So there is all the more reason why he lives in
every human being's love, however unnoticed or onesided
this is. A loving human being has a share in this divine/
human Being of Love. On occasions when people are feeling great love and they speak about being in the seventh
heaven — this is an expression of that experience.

Whilst in a coma a seriously ill patient experienced the
love of the nurse caring for him as a nourishing stream of
light, flowing through and purifying his blood. On returning to consciousness he said: 'Now I know what love is.'

Acceptance of a person opens the way for
angelic guidance

Every time a person is privileged to feel positively accepted
by another the Being of Love begins to work in that person.
The angels steer circumstances so that decisions can be
taken which affect destiny.

The behaviour of a class 12 pupil was such that most of

his teachers were of the opinion he should not be allowed to sit the final school exam. They thought it would be better if life were to present him with a practical challenge rather than that he should have a further year lazing away his time in a senseless existence. A meeting was arranged for the penultimate day of the school year to discuss what should happen to the boy. I was sitting in the outer office for, contrary to my usual habit, I had postponed writing end of year reports until the last day. I myself was amazed that I had done this. Whilst I was sitting there writing, the door to the teachers' room opened and a teacher emerged to have a cigarette. As I ranked as a part time teacher I did not belong to the college of teachers. I asked what the emergency meeting was about and he told me that they were discussing what should happen to a pupil who was about to leave the school. When I heard the name of the pupil I said: 'I could say a great deal about *him*. I have known the boy since his christening.' When the college heard this, I was asked to come in and speak to the meeting. I told the others what was really going on in the boy's soul life, what problems he had in his family, and how he often felt he was in the wrong place. 'If you were to make him leave school now he would be left with a feeling of hatred towards the whole of his school days.' I said all this out of love and positive acceptance of him as a person. The teachers then asked me if I would be prepared to take the boy on and become a kind of mentor for him. I said that I would gladly do it if a second teacher with knowledge of the exam subjects would support me. The German teacher was willing, and so I agreed. On my way home I met the boy. I recognized at once that there was guidance in this, and I told him all that had happened. What a good thing it was that I was writing my reports so late and that I had joined the teachers' discussion. The boy was radiant. There were no further problems with him throughout the coming year, and he did well in the exams.

A Christmas experience

There will be times in anybody's life when a person longs for love, both to receive it and to give it, feeling forsaken by all human love. At such times we can either dissolve in self pity or say to ourselves: 'Nothing is preventing me myself from loving!' When one feels thus deserted by all instances of love, can one command love?

During my training years I had to do my practical in a totally unknown town having just separated from my sweetheart. So I felt the loneliness particularly painfully. I was living in a very big, scantily furnished room with a small stove which hardly warmed it. It was Christmas Eve. I knew no-one in the vicinity with whom I could have celebrated Christmas. Pain and desolation threatened to overwhelm me. However, for some years I had been cultivating the habit of interceding on Christmas Eve for everyone who had to carry responsibility, also for those who suffered and were at this moment in hospital, or in an institute for the homeless, or sitting beside a deathbed, in prison or in a prison camp. I prayed for those in my religious community, in my place of work, and for my personal friends and members of my family. I was not thinking particularly of love, but every intercession contains love. When I had finished, sadness was just about to rise up in me again. But at that moment I felt the door opening. Someone came in and put an arm round me to comfort me. I did not see him, but I knew who it was. It was the Being of Love. After he had gone I felt the truth of Christmas in which the birth of the Christ takes place in an infinite number of ways, but always in the spirit of love.

To love Christ

Two thousand years ago, after the resurrection, Christ asked the apostle Peter three times: 'Do you love me?' And three times Peter ansered: 'Yes, you know that I love you.' Thereupon he was three times given the task: 'Feed my sheep.' Human beings can love the Christ by showing concern for other people, for the sheep and lambs of Christ, for all those whom he loves. He does not live today in human form but in everything to do with human beings on earth. The earth itself, as the abode of human beings, is filled with him. It must last until human beings have transformed it into a star of love, a Christ Star, which will shine spiritually just as the sun shines physically today.

Nowadays, to love Christ also means to love the earth. Today the very tender beginnings of responsibility for the earth and for humankind are just starting to make themselves felt, yet these beginnings are opening doors for angels to be active in human insight, love and action on behalf of true humanity and of the earth. The souls of the dead can also be helpers in this awakening, in this mediation.

Angel guidance on journeys to Israel

For a long time I had persisted with the thought that, like so many other people, I was not going to visit Israel. What was happening there, both with regard to politics and tourism, would only spoil my relationship with the country in which the Christ had lived as a human being. I wanted to keep it as the Holy Land of the Gospels. But one day a colleague said to me: 'While I was clearing out a cupboard in my office I found a folder and put it in your pigeon-hole. Look and see whether it can be thrown away.' I took the folder home with me and looked at it in a quiet moment. It contained diary notes of a visit to Israel. I did not know who had written them. I read my way through them, and was touched by a particular passage. The writer had described the millennia-old olive trees at Gethsemane. When I came to the end of the diary I found a signature written very small. I knew immediately by the writing who had written the diary, and was amazed. The signature belonged to a great-uncle of mine who had died three months before in São Paulo. He had lived there for decades and had only made short visits to Europe and none to me for a very long time. How did his diary get into that cupboard? I asked everyone who might have known. The riddle is still unsolved today. I realized, however, that it was a clear call, and that I should drop my prejudice and go to Israel. I told my story to a friend, and we went there together. We reached Jerusalem in the last week of our journey. After we had moved into our accommodation we went a few steps through the Damascus Gate to the Arabic Cemetery. I was spellbound by the view of the Mount of Olives we could see from there. My friend went on, but I remained there. It was the time between day and night, and dusk was descending. The olive trees, the dark and slender cypresses, the Russian church with its golden cupolas, the impressive roadway lit by neon lights winding its way round the mountain towards Jericho. This view, I did not know why, made a deep impression on me. A while later an inexplicable emotion took violent hold of me. Tears flowed. I fell on my knees and wept. Then I heard within me a voice speaking from very far away: 'Can you not keep watch with me for an hour?' This was what had rivetted me to the spot, the view of Gethsemane, where those words sounded forth for the very first time to the three sleeping disciples. Christ was struggling not to die before he had fulfilled his task of dying on the cross. I accepted his words as a message to me personally and was amazed how right he was. When indeed did I keep watch with him? My awareness of his constant presence was in a state of sleep almost all the time, especially in crucial moments. How right he was to ask me that question. I rose to my feet and would have liked most of all to have gone straight home. But now I knew why I had to come to Israel and to Jerusalem. My friend noticed that something special had happened to me, but I could not yet speak about it. We lived throughout the journey without a radio or a newspaper, not knowing what was happening in the world. When we reached home again we heard about the catastrophe at Chernobyl and realized how panic-stricken and upset people were. In fact the whole earth could become contaminated, diseased and destroyed for good, and all before humanity will have achieved our goal of bringing the earth to the point of radiating with love. I calculated that the day on which the Chernobyl disaster occurred was the day on which I had had my experience. As soon as I realized this, the message concerning the earth and the Christ, the Spirit of the earth: 'Can you not keep watch with me for an hour?' acquired a significance far beyond the personal level. Just as he struggled then not to die before he had fulfilled his task of dying on the Cross in the body of Jesus, he is struggling now in the body of the earth that it will not die before it has become a Christ Star, a Star of Love.

Twelve years later I was staying in Jerusalem again for a few days, alone. The town lay in a reddish sand cloud, blown there from the desert on the south side. One could not see far. A reddish fog also hid the view of Gethsemane when, remembering my previous experience, I hoped to see it again from the Arabic Cemetery. It was uncanny, and yet I was not afraid. When on Friday evening, the beginning of the Sabbath, I went down from the Mount of Olives to the valley of Kidron, I met nobody. I was quite alone. There was only a Russian priest who caught up with me and called to me in English asking me whether I knew that it was dangerous to be on this road alone at this time of day. I called back in a friendly way saying that it was too late to do anything about it. By then I already had a direct connection with the world of the angels via the mediator who brought angel messages to me. Prior to this visit the angels had called upon me to entrust myself to them in Jerusalem and, without a definite goal, but just following my feelings, follow the paths along which they led me. After the trip they conveyed the following message to me:

'Israel radiates light. Not by chance did the Christ choose this land. By living his life there he confirmed the special nature of the land. Through him this quality has become much greater. The paths Irene chose at random were the paths Christ had trodden. To this day they still radiate light and warmth. They are marked as though in gold on the spiritual map of Israel. Over the whole of Israel there are signs of his light shining out of the earth. Irene went over the spot where the Cross stood. (This is not in the Church of the Holy Sepulchre.) She walked that way. She became particularly exhausted in the places where the Christ had been exhausted. These places still make people exhausted today. The places where Mary is supposed to have been born and buried are not the right ones, but Mary often rested there. They are places filled with energy; they are uplifting places, because Mary filled them with light. Irene was definitely guided by angels whilst in Jerusalem.'

Although nothing unusual happened to me during those days I clearly felt the proximity of angels.

Being led by Christ to experience angels

Not long after this a totally new association of ideas occurred to me. In past times human beings were led to the Christ through experiencing angels, as we know from the stories about the shepherds in the fields of Bethlehem or about some of the saints such as Joan of Arc. Those who encounter angels consciously nowadays have made way for the Christ within themselves, even if they have not undertaken in the earthly sense to develop Christ qualities in their own being or in their way of life. I, too, had in this sense brought Christ forces to life in me and had experiences of Christ even if these were not actual meetings such as I was privileged to have in Jerusalem.

Nowadays the Christ leads human beings to bring the angels into their lives, to include angels in the life of humankind. If you make way for the Christ forces you can experience a connection with angels.

His being is of the nature of the ego, as we see in a sevenfold picture in the Gospel of St John:

> I am the bread of life.
> I am the light of the world.
> I am the door of the sheep.
> I am the good shepherd.
> I am the resurrection and the life.
> I am the way, the truth and the life.
> I am the true vine.

In our identity with ourselves there lives this higher Ego Being of all human beings, as we wanted to show in the first chapter. His being is of the nature of the Word, as described in the beginning of the Gospel of St John: 'In the beginning was the Word, and the Word was with God, and the Word was God. The same was in the beginning with God. All things were made by him; and without him was not anything made that was made. In him was life; and the life was the light of men. And the light shineth in the darkness; and the darkness comprehended it not.' A few verses further on it says: 'And the Word was made flesh, and dwelt among us, (and we beheld his glory, the glory as of the only begotten of the Father) full of grace and truth.' Nowadays the Christ approaches human beings in everything that speaks to them, i.e. in everything we described in the second chapter. He is active in everything that takes place between people just as it says in the words: 'Where two or three are gathered together in my Name I am in their midst' — I am among them. Where people take up a connection with something living he is between the one and the other. And he lives in the intervals of time, in the free spaces human beings make for him. Thus he also lives in powerlessness, and in every human being's creative activity.

All these realms where Christ is active are filled with his divine Being of Love.

You can of course make the objection that there are innumerable accounts of angel experiences where people have not particularly cultivated Christ qualities. The book market is inundated with them. Also with accounts of near-death experiences. These experiences belong, however, specifically to the people concerned, and are a part of their destiny. They serve the purpose of awakening people's consciousness to an awareness of the existence of a super-sensible world. After centuries of persistent materialism it is high time for this, if humanity is not to fail in its mission and, acting against the ordering of the world, destroy itself and the earth. Waking up is the first act on the stage of today's human drama. The next thing is to live consciously with the Christ forces which are there in us, and work with them to bring about transformation. Because the Christ lives in earthly humankind he is closer to us today than the non-earthly angel beings who can inspire, protect and accompany us only from the supersensible realm, and only then when we grant them access. When an enlightened theologian heard that I was conveying angel messages she said, with horror: 'Angels, oh, we have finished with those!' To which I replied: 'I believe they are still to come!' With her attitude my theological acquaintance will certainly not have any angel experiences, for the angels will respect her freedom, and they need the substance of human trust, human openness to the supersensible realm, in order to be experienced by us.

Merely through the fact of being human we are all connected to the Christ, even if we do not notice it, whereas the angels have to be granted entry. Where our relation to them is concerned the words of Christ apply: I am the door. This is the door through which one human being may enter another and through which angels may also come.

In answer to my questions my attitude was confirmed by the angels with the message: 'A human being can have a great variety of relationships to his or her angel, ranging from none at all to actual communication. The more consciously and sensitively you lead your life the more influence an angel can have on you. Their task is to accompany you along the way. Christ receives greater acceptance among human beings than angels do. Angels remain in the spiritual realm and perceive a human being's soul and spirit. The angels follow their own laws. These laws are given from above downwards. In fact angels are responsible for your soul and spirit, whereas the Christ shares the earthly life of human beings.'

Part II
MESSAGES

How my relationship with angels began

First conversations

One day a woman much younger than myself asked to have a conversation with me. Her name was Agnes. Agnes wanted to hear the judgement of an older person on some totally new experiences she had been having over the past year. She wanted to know whether she could take them seriously, and what she should do about the situation. She had no doubts herself, but she needed an outside opinion. Then she told me that she had been having supersensible perceptions and saw angels both in response to her call and also often when uncalled for. During the Christian Community service she had seen an aura of light descend on the congregation and also on to each individual person. She calls this 'blessing'. She saw an angel on each side of the altar, as though they were keeping watch. During communion she saw the people's guardian angels. During the service she saw the host shining almost all the time. In the Christian Community the atmosphere during the mass was more peaceful than in the Catholic Church. But there, too, a blessing descended on the congregation. Even if a priest was unworthy the angels of the community gave their blessing. An angel had come to her with a pair of scales. The Catholic Church was in the one pan of the scales and the Christian Community in the other. They were in balance, for what counted was the devotion of the faithful and not their abstract knowledge. Among other things the service was also nourishment for her marriage angel. Afterwards this shone particularly brightly. There were a great many different kinds of angels. Although they were not of different sexes they nevertheless had either more of a masculine or more of a feminine character. Agnes was of the opinion that she had not been given this ability for her own sake. She saw angels while in a state of full consciousness and could distinguish between what she herself thought and what an angel told her through thoughts and images.

I asked Agnes whether it was tiring to translate a supersensible content into our language. She said it was a matter of producing the other state of consciousness and not putting anything of her own into it. This required concentration, but it was not specially strenuous. Yet it did require intense preparation and 'inner purification'.

It was clear to me that the person who was speaking to me was completely sound, with both feet on the ground, and that she belonged to those people of whom Rudolf Steiner already spoke at the beginning of the twentieth century as being people who would be appearing as the first witnesses of a change of consciousness in humanity.

Agnes lives in the country. She has a family, practises a profession and leads the life of a modern person. She has practised meditation for many years. I corroborated the truth of her experiences. After she had left, the question occurred to me whether I should work with her at some time?

Six months later Agnes got in touch with me again. She told me that the angel of the community wanted to speak to me. I went with her to the chapel and received messages there showing me in which directions the community was on the right path and where it still needed to alter and learn things. Without seeing the angel, I could clearly sense the presence. It was a moving episode which affected the whole of my future life. The conveying of the angel of the community's words through Agnes took place in full waking consciousness, i.e. not under hypnosis, nor in a trance nor through channelling, as often happens nowadays, where it is not at all clear who it is who is speaking through a medium. Elisabeth Kübler-Ross, for example, describes such a case, where she also did not recognize who was there.* Spiritualistic phenomena must not be confused with genuine spiritual encounters, either. Spiritual beings have to be perceived spiritually and not materially. Human beings can raise themselves into their sphere by way of meditation and prayer.

Meditation is a heightening of day consciousness, an awakening on a higher level. Since this first meeting I have kept my connection with angels.

The angel of the Christian Community in Moscow

Before one of my visits to the Moscow community which I was in charge of I asked whether the angel of the community wished to tell me anything. The answer gave me tremendous strength for my work there. I was told that angels would welcome me most joyfully in Moscow. The name of the angel of the Moscow community was 'Goodwill' and that of his servant 'Golden Light'. He had a great many more angels serving him. Even if from an earthly point of view everything still looked weak and unremarkable, all my work there up till then had been a sowing of seeds in good soil. The angels were caring for them. It would be a long time before they sprouted into life, but now was the time for sowing. I should pay attention to the signs the angels sent in Moscow. On my first day there, while I was travelling on the underground, my gaze fell on a quotation

---

*See *The Wheel of Life* (Bantam 1988).

that was set out in both Russian and English high above a window. It said: 'It is so easy to abuse an angel. They show their open face like the blind. Be courteous. They expect it. That precisely is the gift of angels visiting our kind.'

I was very startled. I had imagined I had not seen anything of the big reception I had been promised from the angels. And then I received this sign in the Moscow underground of all places. My whole time in Moscow contained, in contrast to before, no tension whatsoever, and was rich in spiritual substance. Shortly after my return home I received a message from the angels of which I may perhaps give some excerpts. First of all I was told that I had noticed only a small fraction of what there was to be noticed of the things which had been prepared for me, which had been more of a personal nature. However, the community angel and his helper were very happy about what had arisen in the community.

The angels make contact with me

Again, a while later, I was spoken to by angels. Although it happened through the agency of Agnes yet I had a direct experience of it: 'Forming a connection with you is a joy to all of us. The last thing we want to do is criticize.' This was followed by a description of my character which I fully recognized. Then came the request: 'Make a note of all your questions. For your own good we cannot answer all of them. Even we ourselves have to withdraw from some areas and leave it to the course of the world and to higher powers. But you will in any case let your conscience put the questions to the test, and then we will put you to the test. We will not answer silly questions. Nor questions to do with time — for time plays a different role for us. Please take notice of the opportunity. We have been waiting for it and working towards it. Things that interest you and are for everyone's good should not remain unasked. We would like to encourage you in this direction. This will not make excessive demands on Agnes.'

A period of rewarding co-operation began. But I had to create the right condition for all the messages by asking questions or sometimes even not asking them. Freedom is the principle on which angels associate with human beings.

What is suitable today and what is not

Messages received in trance are not for today

For a long time I had been in the habit of testing reports of supersensible messages, of which there are an abundance today, and not rejecting or accepting them on principle. I asked the angels about a case of this kind. The answer was: 'You were absolutely right in realizing that this book is rubbish. Trance is a shady method. One should not work with it. The actual spirit leaves the body and, sad to say, anyone can play a trick with it. There are very few people whose only way of reaching angels is by means of trance. But that has more to do with the state of their own soul/bodily constitution. It is difficult to describe. These people were chosen to be mediators, but they are too weak. Neither in body nor in spirit could they bear speaking to us directly. It is important to be inwardly centred. But do not be misled. Trance messages no longer belong to this day and age. The spirit has to remain in the body. That is most essential. The spirit has to be awake. In trance the spirit leaves the body and goes to sleep. That cannot be right.'

Reactions to angel messages

Just as from the aspect of the evolution of humanity as a whole there are certain kinds of connections to spiritual realms which are unsuitable for the times, so can this also be the case where the evolution of individual human beings is concerned. I spoke to very few friends of mine about my new relationship to angels. Some of them reacted sceptically. Others asked whether they might also on occasion ask questions. So I passed these questions on. The answers varied. In the first case the angels said: 'This question has to do with the man's absolutely personal karma. He needs this problem and has to sort it out for himself. We shall not give an answer.'

In the second case they said: 'Only mature well-rounded people can get in touch with us. This person has not got the strength to cope with us. We hold a mirror to people and also make demands. It is not always gratifying to associate with us.'

In the third case they said: 'This person is someone who has an angel guiding him. A different relationship to us is too much for him and also for us.'

Marriage

In response to a question as to whether marriage was indissoluble I was told: 'It will have to be weighed up. There is no clear Yes or No. It really has to be decided afresh in each case. In some cases divorce and re-marriage are necessary, but only the higher powers know the answer. It is very, very difficult for a pastor to give advice here. As distinct from earlier times the present gives the opportunity of living through several past karmic connections. Therefore, in contrast to before, there are now changing love relationships, more divorces and so on. Yet this does not at all indicate that people are too happy-go-lucky! On the contrary! There are a lot of borderline cases which require painful decisions. This is all part of the turn of the millennium. Separation and the entering into a new relationship has nothing at all to do with human freedom. You can be free only if you find your spiritual counterpart. Otherwise you are imprisoned by changing weaknesses. A lot of people do not realize this. What is human freedom alto-gether? That would be a chapter in itself.

'In the present difficult time of transition old laws apply. For this short phase we cannot issue new laws. There is a discrepancy. Humankind has to find its way back to the old laws. And just after this present turbulent time they will find them again. At the present time marriage is dissoluble, but this period of many marriage relationships will come to an end.'

People have to make their own decisions

A Russian woman who had to shoulder great responsi-bility and faced a difficult decision requested me to enquire whether she could ask for help in making this decision. Agnes saw quite spontaneously a negative shake of the head. Later on she was given the following mes-sage to pass on: 'To B.R. It is not true that we are telling you nothing. We are happy about any request for infor-mation. It is just that we must not make the decisions for human beings when it concerns important human deci-sions. People should listen with their inner ear and antici-pate knowingly what should take place. We see the trouble you are taking and support you as much as we can. But do not forget that we are "only" angels. We can only think about spiritual things, not things to do with humanity and the world. What we can tell you is: have a clear inner ear. And when you hear: I need more peace, then take more time for yourself. Otherwise you will get ill. Listen to the inner call within you. It means a lot to us. That is how inner understanding comes about. You only hear inside yourself. So listen! We are with you. Always. Do not forget that! Your angels.'

Universal memory

Angels give direct answers to very few human beings. And most of these answers contain instruction that applies in general. Someone told the angels that there was a woman in his village community who claimed to remember experiences from past lives which were intimately connected with the life and passion of Jesus. She also said that most of the people in the village had had an incarnation as an Essene. 'Is this true?' he asked. The answer was: 'You did not live on earth in Jesus' time. Nor were the other people in the village with Jesus during his short life. What the woman is seeing is what is called universal memory. That is, everything that has happened, is happening now and will happen, is preserved. It can be recalled. You then see it all as if you were part of it and were involved in what was happening. But you are not really there, and were never there in a bodily form. There are a great many approaches to these things. We show them to some people in a dream. Some people are barred from seeing it because it is still too soon for them. Others have access to all this information because they receive it, experience it and work with it consciously. There are a great many more variations regarding the universal world memory. In this small circle of your village community a few of them were in religious communities, in later branches of the Essenes or sects with different alignments. That is not significant. In Jesus' time this woman had a different function. She was not incarnated. This woman finds it very difficult to place the various items of information she receives.'

Questions about reincarnation

There was a question about whether a well-known authoress had been Anne Frank in her last life, as she herself thought. In a publication about these matters she had caused a considerable sensation and intense discussion.* As a child her parents had taken her on a visit to Amsterdam. Without ever having been there before she showed them all the places where Anne Frank had lived. In one of her books she describes later how she was baited and slandered by certain people. At the end she finds out in a dream that these people who were attacking her emotionally with such violence had been her concentration camp executioners in her past life.

The angels see this quite differently. Their answer was: 'This woman was not Anne Frank. It can happen that unborn human souls accompany spiritually a human being who is going through a very distressful destiny. They experience everything as deeply as though it concerned themselves. This woman was such a soul. She had become connected so deeply with Anne Frank before birth that today she feels she identifies with her.'

The angels also explained the following: 'A lot of people who feel today that they are reincarnated holocaust victims are not. There is a universal memory into which people can look today. A lot of people then think it was they themselves who experienced what they see. They lack the correct concepts for it. Holocaust victims have by a long way not returned in such large numbers. Their return will be spread out over long ages. Humankind would not cope with so much difficult karma all at once.'

---

*The book referred to is: *And the Wolves Howled* by Barbro Karlén (Clairview Books 2000).

Regarding the holocaust the angels also said: 'In all epochs terrible crimes such as these have been perpetrated against human beings, and are still being perpetrated against them in many parts of the world. But what happened in Germany was a second crucifixion of Christ.' On hearing this Agnes saw a great many deadly arrows over the whole earth, and in Germany she saw a huge cross reaching up to the sky.

Genuine karma and regression practices

Someone asking about the karmic background of his present life received the following reply: 'We have sent souls to specific countries. You must imagine a plan being made from above. Who is sent to which country? Where is which level of evolution, which level of consciousness? Which souls have to meet which souls? Which country has the best conditions for their karma to be sorted out? And human souls who are further developed also have a right to a voice in decision-making in the spiritual world. One cannot put this properly into earthly words. Our way of speaking is so different.

'You want to have one of your incarnations described in detail. Yes, of course a number of them exist. You know that. But we do not play with such things. You are free to ask. And when the time has come we shall approach you. It is like it is when children cannot wait for Christmas.'

Such messages give us a great deal of basic information, e.g. that not everything described as a view back into earlier earth lives, either clairvoyantly or through a method of regression, is necessarily of the lives of the people concerned. There are a lot of mix-ups in this area, and by no means everyone who reaches the sphere of universal memory is mature enough to read it properly. We realize too that the matter of earlier incarnations is not a game. And another very basic thing is that it is very difficult to put angel messages into human language. If such messages are to be conveyed in a conscious state of wakefulness and not via a medium who writes in an unconscious state—which the angels reject today—the angels can only make use of the language, the images and the soul possibilities of the people through whom they wish to make themselves known. In the case of Agnes she is a person who is both interested in the spirit and open to it, yet she is not attached to any spiritual stream or religious community. She is completely a child of our time, taking as much interest in outer spiritual happenings and phenomena as in the spiritual processes which are becoming more and more accessible to humankind today. That the angels are reserved in many respects is evident in the fact that their messages do not have the least tendency to sensationalism, as has so much in this area nowadays. That despite this some of their messages are being published will be explained in the final chapter. It is happening at their request.

Various ways of relating to the world of the angels

The angels once explained to me why Agnes had this ability while I, and others who would certainly deal with it in a proper way for our time, did not have it. They told me that before birth we each decide with our angel how we shall communicate with one another. Today, though, there are still very few people who remain bound to their pre-natal decision. The angels once added the following: 'Human beings are led by angels. Human beings would be wise to realize this. Their path often appears to be without illumination or sense. Yet the goal explains everything. The connecting link binding us to a human being is often very thin and full of sadness. Human beings no longer hear us. This is why it is now their task to raise their consciousness to the supersensible level. Human beings must be aware of us again. Otherwise there will be no way ahead for them. They will lose their bearings. Why is it that some people perceive us as thoughts and ideas, while others see and hear us? Letting us in, wanting to see and hear us, and the matter of karma, is all connected. We make ourselves invisible so as not to confuse them too much. Some human beings cannot stand having "visible angels" constantly around them. Agnes, too, was not granted these experiences earlier on. She could not have coped with them. Irene, who made contact with us through Agnes, decided before birth, with the three angels belonging to her, to live without clairvoyance. She wanted to plunge right into earth existence and discover how a person can remain connected with angels nowadays without seeing them. She did not leave a foot in the door but let it close altogether. She and we denied ourselves any communication either directly or through the sight of one another.'

Distorted messages from angels

A book once came my way in which a woman conveyed angel messages to other people. Some of it struck me as being similar to the messages I received through Agnes. But the whole book showed clearly that it was written for a definite purpose. The reader was meant to become convinced of a certain world view and to be introduced to the importance of its representatives.

I asked the angels what they thought of it. The answer

was: 'There are chapters in this book which we would prefer to see as blank pages. Unfortunately these are not angel messages but personal interpretations of the authoress. In fact, the risk is always there that personal opinions will intrude. How can this happen? You should go on writing only as long as you can keep your concentration enough to continue to put everything to the test. But if you are deaf in one direction then you are blind too. And then these mistakes happen. When we are quoted as being the authors of the whole book it is quite wrong.'

In response to this I asked why the angels speak to such a person at all. I was told that it had already been arranged between that human being and the angels in the pre-natal condition that they would speak to her and she would have the faculties for it. But human beings often behave contrary to this decision. After all, it is happening under different circumstances. People often behave contrary to what they arranged with their angel before birth. The results of such discrepancies have to be borne. Yet the angels remain true to their decision with the risk that human beings misuse their freedom and forget and deflect their own decision.

I had to think of the writing in the Moscow underground, beginning with the words: 'It is so easy to abuse an angel.'

Freedom and necessity

Agnes once gave me the job of telling someone I was fond of something very unpleasant and persuading her to forgo something. I found this extremely difficult, and I was told: 'You have to struggle with things you find unpalatable. You are wondering why you have to concern yourself with something like this. Well, certain things are up to you, and when you ask us for our advice we give it to you. This time you don't like it. You are not obliged to follow it. But be glad that such things happen. This is the only way to get to know people. And wasn't that what you always wanted?'

How Agnes perceives angels

When I asked Agnes what it was like when she perceived angels she wrote and told me: 'When an angel wants to be perceived he fixes his eyes on me. It feels the same as when a person stares at you. You look up from your book or your work and look in the direction from which the stare is coming. I am aware there is someone in the room, but I do not know, before I turn round, whether it is an angel, three angels, my dead father, my son's teacher or someone else. The presence can be felt, like the presence of a bodily human being. Angels give advice. They are messengers. Once, an archangel was present. The air gets so dense, so full, it makes you afraid. You have the feeling you are being overwhelmed, you are not able to breathe any more. Mother-of-God beings have also been present, that is, helpers of hers. I was afraid of really looking at them. I have a feeling that is a level to which I cannot raise myself. How does one perceive them? In my daily meditation angels come to explain things, to ask for help and to complain. When one is alone in very peaceful moments one perceives them very well. When one gives them leave they are always present. It works best when one goes away alone on holiday. Angels have very different emanations and also look different. The community angel of our village has an energy like the light in a dome. Their emanation is feminine or masculine, even childlike. And one usually knows which one one is dealing with. You recognize them.'

Angels perceive human beings differently from the way we do

In the conversations Agnes had with angels it would frequently happen that different angels were called according to which one was responsible for the particular area to which the question referred. The leading angel of our time, Michael, is almost always present, also during the service of the Consecration of Man. Agnes has no fear of him. He belongs to the questions that are answered.

You have seen from these descriptions that it is not only angels and deceased souls who can be perceived in the spiritual realm but also the spiritual being in the body of a living person. These also come to Agnes sometimes to ask for help, without the people knowing anything about it themselves in their day consciousness. And when they have been given angelic help they thank her and disappear again from Agnes' sight. From this description we understand that the words with which an angel greets a human being are always: 'Fear not!' whereas Christ's greeting is: 'Peace be with you!' Whether a person is granted a conscious connection with angels is not decided according to human standards. It does not depend on how well or badly people meditate, pray or do their spiritual exercises. These exercises have an effect on one's destiny only if one does them without a view to what one will gain through them in the way of success, progress in one's development, and so on.

Regarding a person who considered himself utterly weak in all his spiritual exercises the angels said they could take up a connection with him because his whole life had been a prayer. His caring or loving thoughts about another person had already been in the nature of intercession. Only the angels themselves know when one is mature enough from the point of view of one's karma to take up a conscious connection with them. They welcome it very much when we thoroughly check the source and content of their message. They do not ask for blind obedience. Those methods belong to their opponents who are endeavouring to dispute their right to help humankind achieve their God-given goal. All those who turn to them while keeping their freedom intact have some kind of unconquerable experience proving this. So it is definitely possible, in the great flood of supersensible experiences we are presented with today, to distinguish one kind of spirit from another.

Questions for which particular angels are responsible

Relating to elemental beings

I asked the angels whether I should work towards seeing the elemental beings whom I could feel around me. The angel called to be responsible for this question was the angel of the English Garden in Munich. He reminded me that I had undertaken for this incarnation not to see spiritually. Apart from this, perception of the elemental beings by means of a 'clair-feeling' was much more appropriate. If we bring them into our own soul images we force them down to a level below the one they are on. Their level is between the earthly and the spiritual level. Marco Pogacnik, in whose perceptions and reports on healing the earth I have taken a great interest, and whom I have spoken to personally, can put himself on their level and can therefore present them not too rigidly in living lines. He also perceives them first of all in feeling. I too should leave it at that. Images would even box me in. Without images I would experience with greater freedom. For quite a while I had experienced the English Garden as a real being, and I was very happy to have entered into a genuine dialogue with that being. The angels had let me know on a previous occasion that although there are landscape angels who do not belong to their realm they do collaborate with them.

The apocalyptic number 666

To the question of what was the significance of the number 666 in the Book of Revelation (which comes round for the third time in 1998) a particular angel was called named Jerome, who said: 'Three times 666, what does that signify? Does a spiritual effect emanate from it? The earthly world can protect itself by perceiving the heavenly worlds. We have been taking the necessary precautions for a long time. Humankind is paralysed, asleep. We are aware of this number. The increasing gravity of a situation of change was no secret. Why shout now all of a sudden? It has been known for a long while.

'How can humankind arm itself—particularly a pastor? By believing in us, strengthening us from below, and sending strength upwards. A great deal of strength will be required, but we have powerful forces at our disposal. The battle will be carried out in other spheres, but the earth will suffer the effects. It is of course up to humanity to transform these effects, to become conscious of them, and be strengthened through the power of God. It is immaterial what human beings call the God to whom they pray. Prayers for peace do a tremendous amount to reduce the veil of darkness, though unfortunately not every human being is aware of this. A time of prayer and inner deepening should come. It is not easy to summon other people to do this. They do not see the help they should be aware of.

'A rose has thorns, leaves, blossoms, seedlings, shoots. Just as human beings do. All together they amount to humankind. We are not taking up the battle unprepared. We know what we have to do. And a web of soul lights is spread out over the earthly globe. The emissions are powerful. We need this force of emission. Amen. When the time comes I shall get in touch again. I am glad someone is taking an interest.'

The following day Agnes added an explanation to this in writing: 'Jerome has hands of fire. I have never seen this in an angel before. They have a fiery emission without combustion. A great host of angels work under him. It was like a kind of performance by him. I know very little about this theme, and I imagine he could answer specific questions himself. Only I am not the person to ask him. Perhaps we should do it together sometime. It is sometimes an effort for me, too, to put these images into words. And I imagine that if you could see them you would aim at other things. Yet I think that somehow it will be all right as it is.'

It is surely justified that these dramatic expectations associated by many people with the end of the millennium are corrected. And it is equally justified that we human beings discover what our task, our contribution could be, what help we have the opportunity to bring to this supersensible event.

A group of people is currently endeavouring to do something in this direction. They are trying to pay attention to positive processes that will bring peace to their lives. They meet once a month and congregate round a lighted candle. Everyone who so wishes tells the others about a similar occurrence and lights his own flame from the candle. Then thoughts are exchanged on the basis of a mantric verse, and we close the peace gathering with a recitation of the Lord's Prayer.

Asked further about this, the angel said: 'Such peace gatherings should definitely be continued. They are visible over a large area. A pillar of light. They remove for the angels a part of the dark clouds round the earth. The angels support this.'

The supersensible School of Michael

That we usually speak of angels and not *one* angel corresponds to the reality. Just as Jerome is surrounded by a host of angels belonging to him, it is the same with other angels who are connected with a specific sphere and take responsibility for it.

There was an occasion when there was a message from Michael and his six helpers:

'About the things of the world. The hierarchies which human beings form here on earth are laid down in the higher spiritual worlds. Therefore it is not by chance who holds which office. The particular person chose it for himself, felt called to it. Why does one happen not to be clairvoyant in the way Agnes is, when it would be of such benefit in one's office? These gifts, too, are wisely distributed. You can be publicly active. You can be quietly active. But you cannot have everything. In the Michael School souls cannot imagine before birth how difficult it is on earth to establish a connection to the spiritual world, how infinitely far and empty of air is the gap which has to be bridged. When the soul sets out to incarnate it is in such a glorious light which, however, gradually fades. And suddenly nothing is left, only presentiments, side-lights, intimations. One loses one's confidence. No-one here can imagine that a human life is so far away from our School, from our world. Even our pupils who have taken up these thoughts into themselves are left with only light veils of mist in their earthly existence. Yet they have to reveal these veils. And we angels do our best to help human beings to have these—if they can stand them.'

This message is about a Michael School in the spiritual realm. The first person to speak about this was Rudolf Steiner. It prepares those people for incarnation who, in the present Michael age, want to open themselves in earthly life to the spiritual world. In our time, which is under the guidance of Michael, the objective is to overcome materialism and to have the experience again of life on and together with the earth as a being filled with spirit. To bring about this progressive step and serve it is the task of those who belonged to the Michael School before their birth. Rudolf Steiner describes Michael, the guiding spirit of our epoch, as the being of 'cosmic intelligence'. Under his leadership the intellectual thinking of present-day human beings will become able once again to be active in the sphere of life, to be aware that the material realm is a condensation, a final stage of a spiritual process. Human thinking has to be transformed in order to include the supersensible realm. The traditional concepts from the past will again become realities; also religious ones such as angels, God, Christ and the Holy Spirit.

Agnes pictures Michael as two intersecting triangles (a six-pointed star), being the image of the Holy Spirit. Michael is in the middle.

Wise statements received

Agnes sometimes simply receives a 'gem' of wisdom which she passes on to me, e.g.:

'Daring has nothing to do with being brave. It is a special form of knowing God. People who are really daring are rare—and they are mostly deeply religious.'

'Life is not a hardship, it is an opportunity.'

'When people worry, their thoughts go round in a circle. They are no longer receptive for the inner voice. It makes no difference whether the worries are justified or not. People who have sound self-knowledge notice this "false" attitude to worries, this "losing your nerve", and thinking in circles. Therefore you should allow worries only a small corner in order to be free for redemptive thoughts.'

Answers to questions about the German folk spirit

The following texts were written down as well as was possible, without any intention of publishing them. So they are fragmentary. Agnes received them partly in pictures and partly in words. We shall show when a new statement begins by putting fresh quotation marks.

The German folk spirit after the Third Reich

'As early as after the First World War Germany was influenced by the whole of Europe. Germany absorbed the whole of the dark, conflict-laden cloud hanging over Europe. The folk spirit became absolutely enveloped in it. The Second World War tore these clouds to pieces and bore them in a series of explosions to other countries. The German folk spirit itself exploded. When the war was over the land was dead. Europe was burnt out. It was a smouldering conflagration. The German people are searching for their folk spirit. It does not exist on earth. Germany is still scorched earth. The folk spirit can return, but the earth is not yet ready. Nothing can arise as yet. Germany is as quiet as after an explosion. This is still the case. Everyone is waiting. The folk spirit can only return if people turn their minds to the spiritual world. It exists, but the time for it is not yet. The picture is as though there had been terrible destruction. When the folk spirit comes it will be like new, a new spirit. Throughout the periods in which it is not there it works much more strongly in the spiritual worlds. It will come only if it is received by the people. Then it will be very strongly outwardly active. Today the German folk spirit is high above Germany. To awaken the German folk spirit in the nation is the work of its own people.'

Israel and the German folk spirit

Another question raised was about the kind of relationship existing between Israel and the German folk spirit: 'Both countries, Israel and Germany, had from the beginning of time the same sounds, the same colours, the same warmth, and earth consisting of the same substances. Because this was so from the beginning the whole destiny of the two countries has gone the way it has. The Jewish people were the first to step into the light. The others were still in sha-dow. The seed which was sown in both lands was the same, but germination was held back longer in the case of the German people.

'The world will go through great change. A great deal has first to be thought, and created on a spiritual level, so that it can happen on earth. Present-day human beings think that it is all too late and that the earth is dying. But thoughts are realities and work in a transforming way.'

'The German folk spirit was blown up by the explosion of the war and aggressions. It hovers over the land; it exploded and is still not yet there. Seen with spiritual eyes the country has been destroyed by fire, laid waste.

'The question as to what connection there is between Germany and Israel goes back a long way. Each nation has its own destiny. Israel's suffering belongs to this, as prep-aration for Jesus Christ. All nations come from one genea-logical tree. Israel and Germany are one branch which has split into two. By the will of God they have developed differently. Their mutual sympathy turned into hate and envy, which is only the reverse form of love. The basic material of their original soul is the same. Yet despite this their development has been quite different. The history of the two nations is so different. In Israel the development of the ego happened sooner. The people of Israel have already got the flower, the Germans have not even got the soil. The blossom was taken from them by the war. What can be done to change this?'

'The pollen for the German seedlings buried deep in the naked rock comes from Israel, and appears as flower. The length of Germany's karma cannot be shortened. It is like the sleep of sleeping beauty, which has its own allotted time.'

'There is a dark cloud over Germany hindering the folk spirit. While the sun cannot break through nothing can grow. The cloud cannot be got rid of yet. It is all so close.'

'The previous generation that participated in some way is still alive. It has to die before the cloud can disappear. That is a law. This holds good in other countries too. The sky grows dark when there is too much sorrow and death. Because of the previous period of not being awake and not sensing what was in the air the German folk spirit was misused. Its own people allowed it to be blown to pieces. A large portion of its people supported it. Not until the departure of the dark cloud, which is already growing lighter, will a new development be possible. There is plenty of life and energy in the mutilated earth, but without the sun nothing will happen. The time has not yet come. Things will not change until the first third of the new century. The people to do it are already there in Germany, but the folk spirit has not yet connected up with them.'

In response to being asked, the angels supplemented these messages about the relationship between Germany and Israel by saying that it is not present-day Israel that is meant with the reference to a flower that will fructify the seedling lying in the mutilated earth of Germany.

Agnes said: 'I see a land in imbalance. Blood is still flowing. That is how it looks at present. But there is also ancient Israel of the time of Christ, and that did not have exactly the same boundaries. Ancient Israel was quite different. It contained something of every part of the world, and this in a concentrated form, which means that you could actually have found everything there. Israel is the spot which is unique in its having everything. Therefore it was the only possible place where Jesus could be born. After Christ died on Golgotha this changed. It became like a collection of things which do not belong together at all. There was no longer harmony there. Dissonances could be seen as though everything was becoming higher or lower. Things are simply not evened out anymore. But at some point it has begun to move to and fro again. There is still movement there, but it is abrupt. It is still not in balance. But these many little things no longer exist. As a country it looks compact. Above this country there live souls who have many times lived on earth as Jews, Israelite souls. This group of souls will incarnate in Germany and through these incarnations, through these seeds, the earth can be broken open again — which is something of which Germany is in such great need. This will happen in the near future.'

The twenty-first century

The question was asked: What will things depend on in the twenty-first century?

'On human souls. To what extent they perceive spiritually.'

'Michael, as today's leading time spirit in the angel world, would be glad if he knew what the next century will be like. It depends on human beings. Michael and his hosts have a very concrete plan, but it is not certain whether this will come into effect. It is a battle that will not take place in this world but will send its vibrations into it like a pendulum. If it swings in the right direction the earth can survive.'

'A plan has been set for the coming century. But due to the battle in the spiritual worlds it can be postponed. At the beginning of the last century it was light, and there were wonderful prospects for the future. Because of the aggression in Europe everything was postponed and destroyed, and it can no longer take effect. The extent of the war could not be imagined beforehand. The coming century is starting off much greyer. Light is there only potentially. Just now it looks dark, but the angels are hopeful.'

With all these messages we can see clearly that the angels are waiting for human beings to become active and responsible, so that they can join forces with them. It is not a matter of human beings obeying the angels, even possibly against their own judgement and wishes. It is really about angels and human beings working together.

The relationship of Christ to Jesus

Again and again I kept wondering what it meant that Christ only entered the man Jesus at the baptism—as Rudolf Steiner describes from spiritual vision—and yet it is said that he experienced a whole human destiny. In that case he must surely have gone through a human birth as well. Similarly, a full human life also includes the experience of human death. Yet in his lectures on the St Mark Gospel* Rudolf Steiner describes how the Cosmic Christ Impulse forsakes Jesus before the death on the cross, in the form of the youth clad in white who flees from the guards.

On the one hand Christ was the only god who experienced birth and death as a human being. On the other hand he only entered into a human body thirty years after birth and forsook it shortly before death.

After barely two years I ventured to ask the angels this question which had been with me for so long. As Agnes has so slight a connection with anthroposophy I received the answer expressed according to her understanding.

The first answer to my question was as follows: 'In the case of Christ Jesus, whose incarnation cannot be compared with an ordinary incarnation, the Christ Ego was fully on the earth before birth, i.e. his innermost soul was in the body of Mary. He entered completely into the earth sphere. At the baptism the Holy Spirit came down and opened his eyes, so that he could then see everything also from the cosmic point of view.'

I then described to Agnes the mystery of the two Jesus

---

* *The Gospel of St Mark* (Anthroposophic Press 1986).

boys as told by Luke and Matthew, with their different genealogy and the different accounts of their childhood. And I told her that Rudolf Steiner had informed us that the individuality of Zoroaster had incarnated in the Jesus described by Matthew, and that the pure part of Adam, the part which had remained in paradise, incarnated for the first time in the Jesus described by Luke. And I went on to tell her that when the occurrence took place which Luke tells us about regarding the twelve-year-old boy in the temple, the Zoroaster individuality entered into the sheaths of Jesus' body, life and soul. And I asked how this relates to the answer given above.

This is the reply she received: 'Matthew and Luke see these boys as two in one. They are one, and yet people could see two. It depends on what one sees or what one is destined to see! It is important to recognize and accept both of them, for the two of them are one. It is hard for the human spirit to realize this.

'It is not the case that the Christ God only entered into Jesus at the baptism. That would have been far too simple. What happened at the baptism was that the Cosmic Christ Ego was brought by the Holy Spirit. That is a further, no, the greatest, most perfect aspect that applied to him. God experienced birth as a man! As a human being! At death he says: "My God, why hast thou forsaken me?" At the gates to life and death Christ was a human being. This rounded off the circle of his human life on earth.'

In answer to my further questions, more information was added on the evening of the same day: 'The Christ Ego lived in both the Jesus boys, formed their body within the maternal body, and went through the birth of Jesus.'

When Agnes asked in return how he could live in two people she was given the following comparison: There was so much to include of what belonged to humanity's destiny, it was like having a chest which is not big enough to take all the contents and therefore two chests are required.

'When Christ became man there were two and yet they were one. Jesus was not the incarnation of Zoroaster and Adam Cadmon. Together with him they formed a spiritual whole.'

Agnes sees a cross. The one beam is Adam Cadmon, the other is Buddha. The crossing point is above Jesus' head. Where the beams cross, above his head, is Zoroaster. Christ himself is the whole cross. 'At the baptism the Cosmic Impulse united with Christ Jesus. It fired him, and left him shortly before his death in the form of the fleeing youth. The Christ God who had become man and who lived in Jesus from birth, also goes through death. The Cosmic Impulse lived in him for three years. That is the Cosmic Will which makes him one with the Father and by means of which the cosmic plan is realized on earth. The Christ Ego entered into him before birth. Cosmic superconsciousness, which has nothing human about it but is divine, remained in the heavens. This cosmic superconsciousness was brought by the Holy Spirit. Before the baptism the human being Jesus Christ had guiding beings, Zoroaster, Buddha, among others. After the baptism he himself was all of it. He possessed all wisdom. He was the Man-God.'

I told Agnes once again what Rudolf Steiner had said about the various conditions applying to the periods of Christ's life and gave her Rudolf Steiner's *Fifth Gospel* to read. Then I asked the direct question: Is it true that the Christ Ego lived in Jesus as his individuality and not that the Zoroaster ego lived in the Jesus of whom Matthew speaks and the Adam Cadmon being in the Jesus of whom the Luke Gospel speaks?

The answer was: 'Christ is the Logos, is *all things*. The seed of fiery light was planted into both the Jesus boys. Yet despite this the divine cosmos continued to exist. The higher worlds would call the Logos the individuality of the Christ. For it is divine. He experienced his own birth as a human being and he saw it simultaneously from a vantage point outside. Zoroaster's individuality was sent down and accompanied and guided the Matthew boy on his way. The Zoroaster individuality was with the boy. The boy was also filled with divine light. At that point the light was of course still weak, faint. Christ dwelt in the boy as a human being. Zoroaster was a human being, a leading one. The part of the Logos which was able to descend to such depths incarnated fully. The tremendous cosmic part of the Logos came at the baptism. It is not a contradiction to say that Christ was Jesus' individuality. The complications this caused are unimaginable. Yet at the same time the individuality of Zoroaster was there as a guide. He also dwelt in the body of Jesus. Yet it was clear from the beginning that he was a companion only for a limited period. But Zoroaster *was* incarnated. That is possible. And it was similar with the Luke boy. We spoke of the fact that Christ experienced his birth as a human being and at the same time saw it from outside. This disappeared of course, for he became a human being, a child, not a god. His consciousness in his childhood was human. His forces developed gradually. And at the baptism the Logos in him was made complete again. You cannot say that the Logos was previously divided. One part of it was incarnated and another part remained in the cosmos. And yet it was so. But this description is too stark. The right word is not there to describe it. It is very complex and full of apparent contradictions.'

Again I set my mind to thinking about these explanations and tried to reconcile them with Rudolf Steiner's descriptions. I passed my thoughts on to the angels, and asked them to tell me what they thought of them. I wrote: 'The world is of course one whole. The fact that we perceive the world of the spirit and the material world as separate entities is due to our present-day consciousness which can no longer perceive that all matter is congealed spirit, spirit in a more condensed state. This condensed condition can be dematerialized again. This occurred for instance when the Risen One entered through closed doors or disappeared from the physical sight of the disciples. Thus the Logos, the all-embracing Being of the Son, the Ego and the Word, could have incarnated into the material being of the man Jesus and at the same time a part of him could have remained in a spiritual state. Thus the two states—condensed spirit and spirit free of matter—could have worked simultaneously as an undivided whole until, through the baptism, the whole Being of the Logos entered a human being for three years. The Christ-Logos lives in the human Jesus at various levels of incarnation. Zoroaster and Adam Cadmon live in both Jesus beings as guides to the growing Jesus. Zoroaster is a great historical leader of humanity. Adam Cadmon is the essence of innocence and purity of heart. They live as the ego and soul being in the two bodies of Jesus, both of which were filled with the Logos, the World Ego until, as Rudolf Steiner describes in *The Fifth Gospel*, the two became one. Being themselves human egos they were filled with the Cosmic Ego of Christ. This is why we must not see all this separated into "either/or", but as dynamic processes interpenetrating each other, a whole in various different conditions. Can the angels agree with this?'

The answer was: 'Yes, you can say it that way.'

After this struggle for clarity and my comparing of the apparent contradictions, I found the following statement in Rudolf Steiner's *Christ and the Human Soul*: 'By speaking of the entry of Christ into Jesus are we denying that Christ was united with Jesus from birth onwards? This is just as little a denial as it is to say that the soul is in a child before the soul, so to speak, comes to being in this child in the course of the third year'.*

---

* *Christ and the Human Soul* (Rudolf Steiner Press 1984).

Some statements about various apostles

Paul

I asked whether Schelling's allotting of the Christian churches to three of the original apostles corresponded to the truth. According to Schelling the Catholic Church has been given its form by the apostle Peter, the Protestant Church by the apostle Paul and the Church of the future by the apostle John. I asked whether we are living today in the age of John, as is often expressed by the term 'apocalyptic age'.

The angels said that at present the spirit of John was not the determining one. I should find out for myself how things were. They would confirm it, if I were first to discover it. A book would soon come into my hands which would put me on the right track.

After receiving this information I took up a book I had bought a few days before, on Christian Rosenkreutz. I had already looked it out before I had got the message. In it was a chapter on the apostle Paul who, believing he was fighting to do the will of God, was working fanatically to destroy Christ. And it was he, of all people, who was given the honour of having a Christ experience which enabled him to become the apostle of the One whom he had been persecuting. He beheld Christ in his present, body-free state. That human beings can have such experiences is something beginning anew in our time. The battle against Christ and everything spiritual as well as the personal experience of the spiritual presence of the Christ belongs to today. Hell and heaven are open.

In a flash I realized: Paul's spirituality determines today's situation. The angels confirmed this.

Judas

On one occasion I received the following information with regard to Judas: 'We are always referred to the fact that Judas' opinion of Mary Magdalene's anointing of Jesus was that it would have been preferable if the money had been given to the poor. Did Judas really say that? No, he thought it, and Christ heard it and responded. Judas was afraid, afraid of the man who knew his thoughts. Therefore it was all the more incomprehensible to him—in view of Christ's spiritual power—that he did not aspire in the end to worldly power as King of the Jews. Judas always had difficulties with talking to Christ who judged him too intently. He was caught in a love/hate situation. Judas could not understand this god, could not imitate his actions. Actually he always remained a stranger with him. When Judas died he was freed at last. It was as though a weight fell from his shoulders.'

The destiny of the apostles

I asked Agnes at a later date whether the apostles and Paul had incarnated again.

The answer was: 'These chosen apostles were human beings. But in the course of their lives their karma was expunged. What was the reason behind expunging human karma? These companions and partly envoys of Christ took on other tasks after their death. In some cases they incarnated again, as there was no reason in every case for karma to be expunged. Some of the apostles (e.g. Paul, still in that lifetime) had times when karma and life's connections were revealed to him. It was like a blackboard from which the chalk was rubbed off, which does not mean that nothing more will ever be written on that blackboard. But not at that moment. When required, a new earth existence might be planned, but from the point of view of karma this was not necessary. There were also apostles whose blackboards were not wiped clean, and who reincarnated. (The blackboard is a picture for plans for an incarnation or karmic plans.)'

I asked her in return whether the apostles were working into the history of humankind, into the evolution of Christianity from out of the spiritual world.

The answer was: 'With regard to the apostles, too, we can confirm your presentiments. They work to mediate spiritual impulses. According to the cycle which is in force on earth the apostles can have an influence on spiritual streams. Particular groups of human beings are under their protection, their influence. And the individual apostles endeavour to improve these streams, to give them a further polish.'

The significance of the Last Supper

On one occasion the angels described how the Last Supper which Christ celebrated with his disciples was experienced from the aspect of the spiritual world. 'The whole of the spiritual world attended the Last Supper. It was like a large white cloud. They were present in spirit. Other beings also. Human beings who were aware of its importance were also present, e.g. certain saints, human beings who were interested in it. They joined the white cloud uniting all the hierarchies. The spiritual world was present in all its might and splendour. That is important!'

Mary

Candlemas

The question was raised as to the actual significance of Candlemas, the second of February, the day on which in the Catholic Church the candles are blessed. It is also the fortieth day after Christmas, the day on which Mary brought the Jesus child to the temple where old Simeon blessed him and told Mary of the sword which would pierce her heart.

What the angels said about Candlemas was that it was a festival in the angel world in honour of Mary. 'A festival whose radiance touched the earth. A lot of music encircles the earth. It is a festival dedicated to Mary, of which the origin lies in the union of Mary with the earth and humankind. Both the feminine/divine aspect and Mary's incarnation are celebrated as a festival, rejoicing over Mary's "life story".'

Why on the second of February?

'The constellation in the heavens is what is decisive. It is on the threshold of a turning-point. The earth's becoming feminine, becoming a receiver, growth is about to begin. The receptive/feminine impulse begins on this "Mary Day". It is the greatest day of celebration of Mary in the higher worlds (except for Christmas). Hands which are open and receptive.'

Depictions of the Mother of God

Before going on a visit to Moscow to the community there, the angels gave me the tip that I should look out for depictions of the Mother of God. I asked them in return if that meant that I should go and look at icons in churches and museums. I would hardly have time to do that. The answer I received was: 'Depictions of the Mother of God are archetypal pictures of the feminine aspect in the spiritual world. These depictions are an archetypal "world image". Older than the two thousand years since Christ's birth. More earthbound. Yet christianized through and through. You do not have to go to churches and museums. She will come to you anyway. You need give neither time not pre-meditation to it. She is there for ever and ever, in the same way as God is. You do not need to go in search of her. She is always there.'

Who is Mary?

The first question I asked the angels about this was whether the two Marys, the mothers of the two Jesus boys, had been reincarnated. I had found nothing in Rudolf Steiner's work about this. I was told that the cosmic feminine element had incarnated just the once in the bodies of the two Marys. It will not be born in human form on earth but lives in all that is feminine, both in every human being, in every woman, as well as in the cosmos. It is the female aspect of the Holy Spirit. This cosmic/feminine being also has dark, evil aspects.

I asked how Mary relates to the archetypal mother Eve and who Lilith is, of whom some people say that she is the part of Eve who remained in paradise and was not driven out. Another tradition says she is the mother of demons.

The answer I was given was that in Eve femininity with both its light and dark aspects came down to earth into the evolution of humanity. In Lilith it remained in the spiritual world, also with its double aspect of light and dark, pure and demonic. Regarding the relationship of the two Marys to one another the angels said that at the moment when the cosmic Christ impulse united itself at the baptism in Jordan with the Logos which lived within Jesus, the virgin being of the cosmic/feminine, which had dwelt for a short period in the Mary of the Luke Gospel who had died young, passed across into the still living mother of Jesus who then, from a spiritual point of view, became a virgin once more. Rudolf Steiner gives a similar description.

The angels then said further that in the spiritual world there were both kinds of beings, those filled with the nature of the Mother of God, and those filled with the nature of the Holy Spirit. World Soul and World Spirit belong together. They beget and bear the Son, the World Ego into all eternity. This happened just once as a physical occurrence.

The immaculate conception

I asked what the truth was about the virgin birth of Jesus, or rather about Mary's conceiving Jesus by way of the over-shadowing by the Holy Spirit.

The angels described it in the following way: 'From a spiritual point of view the conception of Jesus was a great festival. It was a ritual, a kind of wedding ceremony. It also involved human beings. Mary and Joseph were filled to such an extent by the spiritual aspect of the happening that in their day consciousness they could not remember the bodily union. Mary felt as much a virgin as before. That is an immaculate conception. Joseph was the physical father but did not know it. Mary is the quintessence of all women.'

Mary is not an intercessor

On another occasion I was told: 'Mary does not intercede for us, begging God on behalf of human beings to fulfil their wishes and hear their prayers. She is the Mother of Christ living in every human being, the human soul from which is born the Ego of humanity. By looking up to Mary a human being enlivens the Mary quality in him or herself. That is the new way to worship Mary through which the human soul is raised to the soul of humankind, giving birth to the Son, the Christ.'

Mary Magdalene

I asked later about Mary Magdalene. The answer was: 'The woman who anointed Christ's feet was Christ's "spiritual lover". The act of anointing is more than a preparation for death. It is an act of absolute devotion and love.'

The cosmic feminine – the three goddesses

In a course he gave on Celtic wisdom Markus Osterrieder told us that the Celts revered the cosmic feminine as three goddesses: the Virgin Goddess in white, the Mother Goddess in red, the Goddess of death and transformation in black. In Bavaria these three can be found depicted as the three 'Beths' – a Celtic tradition – who have passed into Christianity in the form of three saints. Marco Pogacnik also refers to these three female goddesses, whose colours have such significance in the fairytale of Snow White. The mother of Snow White wishes for a child as white as snow, as red as blood and as black as ebony.

It occurred to me to wonder whether the three Marys in the life of Jesus had anything to do with that.

The answer to this was: 'The three images of Mary compose the cosmic/feminine divinity. Only these three images together make up her whole being. Often several images have to be brought together to make a whole. The Luke Mary represents the virgin, almost childlike picture of femininity, the Matthew Mary, the mother–aspect of femininity, and Mary Magdalene fully completes the picture with her aspect of transformation and the possibility of a dark side this presupposes.'

Is it not true that Mary Magdalene is supposed to have been the great sinner from whom Christ drove forth seven demons? She went through evil, experienced transformation and could stand beneath the cross together with the mother of Jesus and the disciple whom the Lord loved, and experience death with Christ in her soul. Thus she was privileged to be the first person to meet the Risen One on Easter morning. Through darkness, blackness, evil and death she came to the light.

With regard to the black Madonna the angels added: 'The black Madonna has two aspects. It depends what you want to see. The people who flock to her do not go into darkness but into transformation. There are two ways to come through this. The orientation is determined by what you see, opportunity or downfall. Devout people sometimes pray specially to one of these Marys. This image appeals to them—it corresponds to their devotion. The one who ranks highest is the centre of the three.'

Agnes received this picture:

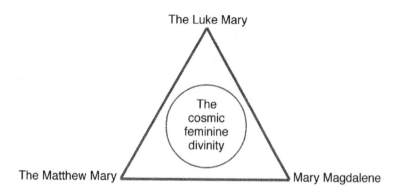

'Each of the three has something of the others in her, but her aspect is the dominant one.'

The three images of woman in the Book of Revelation

In John's Book of Revelation there are also three female beings.

In chapter 12, which is in the middle of the whole revelation, he describes the cosmic woman who bears a child, the Son. She is clad with the sun, has the moon beneath her feet, and wears the crown of the twelve stars. The dragon lurks at her feet waiting to devour the child as soon as he is born. The child, however, is saved by being taken to the Throne of God, and the woman flees into the desert.

The second female being is the whore, the whore of Babylon. She seduces all the great men of this world, kings, merchants and mariners, with her wealth. Yet finally she will be burned and the smoke of her burning will never cease, as it says in chapter 18.

At the end of the Book of Revelation we hear of the bride who has adorned herself for her bridegroom, the Bride of the Lamb, the heavenly Jerusalem. This is humankind, awaiting the return of Christ. She and the spirit cry: 'Come!' and let everyone who hears the call cry 'Come!' The bride here is the being of the community who has accomplished humankind's task, the union with Christ. She appears at the end of the Book of Revelation as the highest ideal. In the middle we are shown the drama of the evolution of humanity. It passes through every kind of seduction. But the fire of purification transforms them to ashes. In the baptism service of the Christian Community ash is addressed as a substance that contains the force of renewal. The cosmic woman is the first image of woman described in the Book of Revelation. I asked the angels whether the three female beings of the Book of Revelation also correspond to the three aspects of the cosmic/feminine. They confirmed this by saying that the woman clad with the sun in the throes of birth is the Mother Goddess, the whore of Babylon is the Goddess of Death and transformation, and the Bride of the Lamb the Virgin Goddess.

The August 1999 eclipse of the sun

Agnes describes five angels at her side, dictating to her the following message: 'Have no fear, for fear darkens your vision! This eclipse of the sun had a strong effect on the spiritual world and the astral body. At important "strategic" points choirs of angels were present (like us five angels), endeavouring with their singing to bring balance and harmony to the earth.'

What effect did the sun eclipse have?

'When the sun disappears and there is darkness in the daytime the spiritual/astral part of the earth enters a vacuum. Our singing and spiritual activity was working to counteract this. Darkness during the day also calls forth evil powers. Under cover of darkness they want to grasp power in areas that are becoming bereft of balance. The fear in human beings attracts them. People who have lost their heads are easy prey. We were also working to counteract that. And there is also a third aspect to consider. Children conceived or born at this time need protecting from inner disharmony brought about by darkness in the daytime. These souls are more susceptible to soul darkness. This sun eclipse could be seen and felt in certain parts of the earth. This also applies to its effects. Yet in order to protect the earth's balance we were distributed over the whole earth. But the effects on human beings were particularly in those areas where it became dark.

'This celestial event is now over. The earth was temporarily asleep, asleep in the daytime, and the astral world was simultaneously in a state of turmoil. The waves of imbalance have become smooth, and the world is now liberated from them. The air is clear of them. And human beings will be capable of thinking more "clearly". This kind of clarity is like a stumbling-block for people. Hopefully they will perceive it as "a thought in which they can awaken". All these spiritual stumbling-blocks are now lying about on earth. The cross is a symbol of them. As soon as a human being stumbles over them they dissolve. A thought then endeavours to germinate in human beings.'

An apocalyptic vision

Agnes experienced something on Good Friday which she described in the following words: 'Today I saw the following pictures during Mass. First of all I saw angels, with Michael leading, all moving towards the front of the altar, to the right of it. After this a picture separated out. To the left there was an infertile, desolate area with an eagle hovering above it. To the right there was a beautiful, fertile landscape. Then I saw people praying and throwing themselves on their knees. Then there came a great tidal wave which bore the people away. There were, however, a few people who stood or sat perfectly upright and remained absolutely untouched by the tidal wave. After this wave had passed, "those who remained" gathered together. They gathered on the shores of the Sun Lake. The sun had come down to earth. It was the Lake of the Sun. They did not mourn for the departed, they were only perplexed, silent and very upright. There were no wounded ones either. People either survived totally unhurt or they were dead.

'Only Mary, the Mother of God, mourned and wept all alone for lost humanity. Her sadness was great. She moved towards the rest of the people who, in the meanwhile, had gathered together, and who wanted to walk forth from the desert to the Garden of Eden. Everything was grey. Everything that our present-day life consists of was in ruins (people, houses, computers, cars). Everything was razed to the ground and completely flat. People just walked over it. Mary went among the people and brought love into their hearts. You could not see Mary, yet you felt her comforting presence. She went to the head of the procession and led it invisibly. The crowd approached a remaining church. This church opened so that everyone could participate in the Mass. It was the Resurrection Mass. The people's great perplexity fell away from them. Some of them were now able to weep. Some of them only now understood. There was also a spring of water there and food. But the people were no longer people. They no longer needed food. Then there were no more pictures.'

How I came to write this book

One day I asked the question as to whether I should write a book again. I gave a choice of various themes, among them the theme of 'angels'. I was thinking in terms of presenting the scenes where angels were referred to in the Bible as archetypal images for present-day experiences of angels. But I was just as drawn to other themes. The following answer came:

'The title of your book has not yet been decided. But one thing is clear; it will be about angels and angel experiences. That theme has been decided. Do you think that all that has happened between us and you has been for nothing?'

I now began to think about how I could conceive of such a book; what could be its inner purpose and design. And I asked the question which I had already been carrying in me, whether I should make use of the angel stories in the Bible as archetypal images for present-day experiences. The answer was:

'Yes, it could be thought of that way very well. But it could also be presented a different way. Perhaps you might take the "archetypal images" into yourself as spiritual support and just describe present-day angel experiences. You should decide intuitively where you want to refer to the Gospels and where not. It is not essential to do so. Could the angel stories not be based on something else? On their names, their messages? What are individual angels responsible for? How do they acquire their names?

'You perceive quite rightly that the Gospels are a tree and the present-day angel stories are the apples on it. But these apples are not connected with the trunk only through the branches and the external image of it but also through the life-giving energy of the tree. This, however, is not visible. Does not this invisible connection, very much felt and heard, exist also with regard to the angel stories? We ask you to think about it. You have such lovely apples!'

I thought about it a little bit. But initially I pushed the theme aside. I told myself that there were so many books about angels nowadays. Why another? Who would have any interest in it? So I put the whole thing aside, and my other work squeezed it out. Then one day an unsolicited message came along:

'The time has come to talk about the book. There is already an abundance of literature on angels giving a helping hand, their messages, their tasks, their hierarchies. We want something different. We want you to write about angels the way you experience them, as something very much alive, something belonging to everyday life. We are not present only when something dramatic happens. We are there all the time and want to show human beings the right way to go. Angel consciousness is in the process of growing, and not a chance thing. Ask questions. It means a lot to us. You are the right person for this book. The rest of it we shall hear from you.'

This appeal made a strong impression on me, of course. I now asked pertinent questions and received very relevant answers in return. One of these was whether I should write in the first person. There were various answers to this.

'The first person is appropriate if it is the truth. Truth gets home to people. Write it as you experienced it. Truth will carry the book and will make an immediate connection with what people experience when reading it. If you know some angel experiences other people have had, then describe it that way.'

I woke up one night and had the feeling I could write the

introduction to this book. So I did. Yet I was still not sure whether this was not too personal and whether it was permissible to speak so openly in this book about my unusual relationship to angels. I asked, and my introduction received total acceptance. It was right that I wrote from out of my own experience and my own soul, and it was important to convey that it had happened to me. I knew the right form every time, because the finished book was there waiting to come forth.

I did not know this at the time, however. I still did not have the slightest idea what I would write, or how. I received a confirmation of my own thoughts which was of great help to me, namely that it is the Christ qualities in us which connect us with our serving angels and, after that, lead us to the Christ.

At my departure, whilst travelling to where I was going to do the writing, I received another morsel of encouragement:

'The book is already within you. Be calm in yourself. Be uninhibited. You will have lots of ideas, you can depend on it. What matters is honesty. Truth will carry the book and bring the message home to the readers. They will feel the truth in it, and this will open them to the angel messages. Do not worry! We are carrying you in our care!'

So this book was written as a kind of commission. The type of people it is intended for are those who can take it up in the spirit of freedom and with real love. May it, in its own special way, strengthen a consciousness of the cooperation between angels and human beings, and contribute towards the christianizing of today's happenings both in everyday matters and in the great events of the ongoing development of humanity. I would like to close with my thanks to the angels.

Epilogue

I want to include mention that Agnes wishes to remain anonymous. This book was not written in order to release a flood of questions to the angels via Agnes. The messages it contains are valid for everyone, and there is enough work to do to refer them properly to one's own life. People may establish a connection to the angels as far as their destiny allows. It lies in the freedom of each individual to accept or reject these descriptions. But it is to be hoped that the accepters and the rejecters will not fight over it but tolerate one another's different natures. Human beings might then be a source of encouragement for angels of peace to become active in the 'war of all against all'. Let this wish of mine accompany the book on its way.